Power to Lead

Power to Lead

Five Essentials for the Practice of Biblical Leadership

Mike Ayers, Ph.D.

ISBN-13: 9780692489727
ISBN-10: 069248972X
Library of Congress Control Number: 2015946877
RBK Publishing Group, Spring, TX

CONTENTS

INTRODUCTION

In 1991, my life changed. I was working as a student ministry pastor at a reputable church in Orlando, Florida, and enjoying a great work environment with good people. Yet, for me, ministry was becoming increasingly empty. A convicting, personal encounter with God during a student pastors' conference caused me to reflect upon my journey in life up that point and where I was going in ministry. It was then that I looked back ten years to a time before I was in a relationship with Jesus. I remembered the lack of meaning I felt in my teenage years, my insecurities at facing life's unknowns, the fragility of my self-esteem, and the fear I felt about death and eternity. Then I recalled the wonderful change that resulted from the decision I made to trust Christ as my Savior. After growing up in a chaotic, alcoholic family and never attending church, at age seventeen I discovered love, purpose, direction, hope, and security in Jesus. It was the most important decision of my life.

The impact of that change and the desire for others to find the same transformation was the reason I went into ministry. Yet, after ten years of vocational leadership in both megachurches and smaller church ministries, somewhere along the way things had changed for me. By 1991, I had forgotten my purpose and mission. I realized I had become more "vocational" in ministry than "called." I also began to look closely at the church. Though I had served in wonderful churches with loving and supportive people, I felt that on the whole, the Christian church in America had become sadly ineffective in reaching those apart from Christ and developing people into authentic disciples. I read Acts 2:42–47 over and over and clearly saw the gap between the church contained in God's Word and the one presently expressed in the world.

I knew deeply that God had designed the church for much more. It was his desire for it to be the most dynamic organism on the planet, and as clearly as anything I've ever experienced, I knew that my calling from that point on was to be used by God to build a New Testament kind of church:

> A church that is a biblically functioning community. A church consumed with the desire to please God in all it does. A church that knows where it is going and why it is going there. A church that responds to God and to each other authentically. A church where spiritually lost people matter. A church where people understand their giftedness and gladly serve others. A church that is creative and contemporary in its expression of God's love. A church that has an understanding of what it's like out in the real world and courageously faces the realities of our time. A church that sincerely worships in awe and reverence for God. A church where the Word of God is the absolute expression of truth. A church where love and acceptance permeates every aspect of church life. A church where pastors and leaders model honesty, vulnerability, courageous leadership and servanthood. A church that is known in the community as the church that cares with no strings attached. A church where excellence is pursued. A church that senses it has a unique destiny and mission from God.
>
> (excerpt from the 1995 Vision Statement of The Brook Church Community)

I believed that one day, this vision would be realized in my life. I determined that I would be different and that my ministry would be different—that, as a family, our household would follow this vision with our full devotion.

So with this heartfelt vision, in 1995 my wife and I, along with four other couples, planted in Northwest Houston what would become The Brook Church Community. I have spent the last twenty years as its pastor.

What I did not consider was that along with the birth of a vision comes the need for the development of the leader who receives it. Coinciding with the work God wanted to do *through* me was a work he needed to do *in* me. God's greater work involved a process for me to learn who I truly was in Christ, the false assumptions I had about "success" in ministry, the exact purposes and values the church must commit to at all costs, and what being an authentic leader truly means. Along with the joys and successes, there have been disappointments and some painful lessons learned, but I am truly grateful for all the experiences that have shaped me, deeply developed my relationship with the Lord, and grown me as a pastor-leader. This work of God and the dear people who comprise it are sources of great joy. I am blessed to be a part of the generous, loving, serving, God-honoring people of The Brook.

I am also grateful for the opportunity I have had to share these experiences and train others in leadership. For the past fourteen years, I have served as a professor of Christian leadership at College of Biblical Studies, Houston. After receiving my PhD in Organizational Leadership in 2006, I was named Chair of the Department of Leadership Studies and was given the privilege to shape our program and its curriculum. What a joy it is to invest in those earnestly seeking to practice biblical leadership!

As you can see, Christian leadership has been my life—but it has also been my passion. I've had the honor to live it, study it deeply, and interact with others seeking to express it. I have seen firsthand the challenges facing young leaders, the vacuum that is left when leadership is not provided, and the incredible power of leadership when practiced authentically in Christ. All this has led me to express my heart and mind in this book you now read.

Power to Lead contributes to today's surging interest in the study of leadership from a Christian perspective, but it also has at least three distinguishing features:

- It offers theology, theory, and practice for leading others from a directly biblical framework. I believe it to be rich with biblical content, and it aims to provide unique insights from God's Word about this important subject.
- It provides a depth to the subject that is perfect for use in the Christian classroom for training in ministry, or for anyone interested in studying leadership deeply from the Scripture.
- It is comprehensive, giving readers a compelling model and structure for understanding and practicing leadership as it emerges from the Bible.

When I speak of "power to lead," I am not talking about authoritative power or a hero-type leader wielding dominance over loyal subjects. I am talking about an inner power that fuels credibility and capability for humble, Christlike influence. I am speaking about an inner strength that flows from prayer, character, faith, and true courage rooted in the calling of God. I am talking about a power to lead that emanates from Christ himself as experienced within and expressed through the leader.

This world seems more confused and upside down with each day's passing. Needed more than ever are humble, willing, and courageous men and women to express power to lead.

I pray this book will be greatly encouraging and enlightening to you.

Mike Ayers, Ph.D.

POWER TO LEAD MODEL

A Model for Biblical Leadership

CHAPTER 1

TOWARD A THEOLOGY OF LEADERSHIP

"For centuries, theologians have been explaining the unknowable in terms of the-not-worth-knowing."
HENRY LOUIS MENCKEN

It is evident, both in terms of attendance and influence, that the church in America is in decline. The number of people who do not identify with any religion continues to grow at a rapid pace. One-fifth of the US public today—and a third of adults under thirty—are religiously unaffiliated, the highest percentages ever in Pew Research Center polling.[1] Researchers George Barna and David Kinneman state that the number of unchurched people (anyone who hasn't been to church in the last six months, excluding weddings and funerals) has jumped from 30 percent of US adults in 1990 to 43 percent today.[2] Likewise, most cultural measures—divorce statistics, out-of-wedlock births, abortions, abuse of drugs, extent of pornography, etc.—indicate the decreasing moral influence of the church.

Research into the deteriorating effectiveness of churches to transform culture and bring new converts into the faith demonstrates that church leaders are ill equipped to address the problems at hand. George Barna asserts that poor leadership is the primary reason for the loss of church impact in America and the chief problem facing the future of evangelical churches.[3] The investigation of R.H. Welch into church administration shows that graduates of seminaries, facing now the realities of ministry, regret that they did not receive more leadership training.[4] In 1996, C.A. Schwartz studied one thousand churches across the globe and found that the formal theological training of church leaders had a *negative* correlation to both church growth and the overall quality of churches.[5] It seems that theological education alone is not enough to make a difference.

The very institutions charged with training men and women to address the challenges of our world through ministry apparently underestimate the need for the study of leadership in that training. Among the ten largest evangelical seminaries in the United States, on average only 12 percent of the courses required for the primary theology degrees (MDiv, ThM) are related to the subject of leadership.[6]

In effect, these institutions convey the message that simply knowing about the nature of God and the doctrines of faith is sufficient for a leader in the church. This steers pastors to exclusively rely upon teaching, doctrine, and theology to mature the church and impact its people. Many ministers first coming out of seminary see their primary role as that of "teacher." However, teaching is not the chief activity they fulfill in day-to-day work. To the surprise of many, pastors and church staff face issues that are challenging and messy, issues that look starkly different from what they were taught in school. As Denham Grierson says,

The "church" so talked about in seminary is neat, tidy and generally civilized. A particular congregation is never neat, sometimes barely Christian and only rarely civilized.[7]

Those who go into ministry end up discovering that the greatest needs of their congregations and the greatest demands upon their time concern functions of *leadership.* This includes such things as inspiring vision in the church, aligning and empowering members in places of service, recruiting and equipping leaders, resolving conflict, building church culture, bringing change, and structuring the church for greater effectiveness. Unfortunately, many in ministry are ill prepared for such aspects of church work.

Jesus came with more than a theological message. He was more than a teacher conveying truth. The Savior embodied his truth, offered experiences that translated it into actual living, and empowered his disciples with a compelling mission that accompanied the communication of the gospel. The redeeming and restorative gospel comes first, but Jesus's life shows that the gospel is not actualized simply by being taught. Jesus influenced people to accept truth and provided a vision for how they could live within it—in other words, he offered effective leadership.

Jesus came with more than a theological method.
He was more than a teacher conveying truth.

Likewise, unless pastors trained in theology also possess the ability to apply that theology and make it effectually alive in the hearts of people, their training will prove inadequate. Church leaders today are in need of authentic and scriptural equipping that provides them with the information and inspiration by which to lead from a biblical perspective. This equipping begins first by understanding that theology and leadership are not mutually exclusive. Rather, the very notion of leadership is embedded in theology from the outset.

God as Leader

The study of leadership concerns the character and motivations of the person leading as well as the dynamics between the leader and others that yield some form of influence. At first glance, this description seems to have little connection to theology. However, upon closer examination, these dimensions of influence prove to connect to the very nature of God.

Well-known theologian and author Charles C. Ryrie defines Christian theology as "the rational interpretation of the Christian faith" and describes the historical, biblical, and systematic approaches to theological interpretation.[8] His practical approach to theology, normal for biblical evangelicals, is where the fusion of theology and leadership begins. Ryrie advocates the idea that theology is not mere intellectual musings about the character of God. Rather, God's attributes are understood in light of how they directly relate to the human context and condition. God has made himself known within this framework, and he has done so for the purpose of glorifying himself by redeeming humankind. This orientation— God-to-man and for a purpose—reflects the very nature of the idea of leadership. When we see this, resulting questions are many: How does God relate to man? By what means? What motivates him to do so? What does he seek to achieve in and through this relationship?

In comprehending the manner in which God relates to man,
we come to understand what leaders should be and do.

God's moral character (indicating his intrinsic goodness), his acts in human history (i.e., his self-revelation consistent with his character), and the purpose for which he reveals himself to man (redemption) possess inherent properties illustrative of leadership. As one with power and authority over humans, God behaves in a way that reveals his loving motivation toward them; he exercises initiative and takes responsibility for them; he clearly instructs them in their responsibilities toward himself and others; he empowers them with the means by which to reach their human potential; and he encourages them through his unending, sustaining presence. God serves as one who equips, empowers, and encourages his followers. Ultimately, who God is and what he does yields influence upon humankind. With intention, he reaches out to men and women to affect them in a way that causes them to recognize his goodness, his eternal purposes, and his potential within them.

These dimensions of God's character and work offer profound insights into a biblical philosophy of leadership. They inform the proper motivations, behaviors, and purposes for which leaders should lead. Said another way, we gain understanding of what leaders should be and do by comprehending the character and motivations of God himself, the kinds of actions he expresses toward human beings, and the dynamics between God and man that generate his influence upon them.

Consequently, an accurate and comprehensive systematic and biblical theology should include some understanding of God's nature as a leader. In fact, I propose that neglecting this aspect of God's character limits our perspective of him. For as we look at the Bible and history, we see that leadership is not only something God *does;* it is by nature a part of who he *is.*

The Bible and Leadership

On occasion I've had theology students in my classes who viewed leadership as a rather unspiritual topic. They categorized it as a worldly concept borrowed from American business culture, and any talk of the subject in Christian education seemed to them unfitting and even fleshly. One student proposed that leadership was a social necessity brought on by the fall and permitted by God only because of the hardness of the human heart. Yet from Scripture we learn that leadership and the need for it is not the result of sin, nor does it conflict with God's intent for man. In fact, the very opposite is true.

Leadership before the Fall

God's actions and ontological attributes reveal him as leader in his dealings with man from the very beginning. His eternal character and consequent manifestations throughout history exemplify traits that all human leaders should pursue because they flow from the noblest intentions, garner the highest form of impact, and reflect the greater glory of God.

In Genesis 1 we first see some of these actions and attributes:

God is good. The creation narrative clearly reveals a moral Creator. The phrase "And God saw that it was good" (Genesis 1:9) demonstrates not only the moral rightness of the created order but also the inherent goodness of the Creator from which it came.

God influences man. The creation account also describes a remarkable predisposition of this good Creator God: at the very center of his heart is a God-to-man orientation—i.e., God reaching out to man and for a purpose. Our creation, and the creation of the world in which we exist, demonstrates our significance and value in God's eyes and that for some reason he is concerned with us and moves toward us.

Why God would create us, seek to relate to us, and love us is difficult to understand in light of his astounding power, authority, holiness, and self-sufficiency. We may feel much like the psalmist: "When I consider your heavens, the work of your fingers, the moon and the stars, which you have set in place, what is man that you are mindful of him?" (Psalm 8:3–4). Yet in the Genesis text, this orientation is clear. It illustrates the great theological premise: "God toward man." This principle of divine orientation is witnessed in God's acts in human history, epitomized in the incarnation of Christ and his death on the cross and sustained through the presence of his Holy Spirit.

An amazing theological premise: "God toward man!"

In Genesis 2, God's leadership of a particular individual demonstrates the God-to-man orientation for the first time. Though in authority over him, the Creator empowered Adam with management over creation, instructed him in how to exist in harmony with God and the environment God had provided for him, and supplied him with what he lacked by blessing him with Eve (Genesis 2:15, 2:16–17, 2:18). These dynamics of *equipping, empowering,* and *encouraging* are at the heart of the idea of biblical leadership.

The orientation of God toward man, for a particular purpose and flowing from a moral motivation, reveals an important picture of biblical leadership. The biblical leader is one of moral character, motivated by love, who acts for the benefit of those he leads in order to ultimately achieve a God-honoring objective. Just as is true of God, the biblical leader has an unselfish and even sacrificial orientation toward his or her followers. Though more powerful than those following and perhaps in a position of authority over them, the biblical leader loves them. This love is not rooted in the deserving nature of the people he or she leads, nor is it driven by what they do in response. As with God, this love is rooted in the character of the one leading. And biblical leaders act on behalf of their followers, thereby providing them with a sense of value and worth as well as the context for them to reach their potential.

God establishes leadership for social functioning. We see the establishment of leadership in the first human relationship even before sin entered the world. Adam was chosen for headship of the original social institution—marriage. As husband, Adam was assigned the role of providing tender leadership to his wife (Genesis 2:19–24; Ephesians 5:22–33). He was to offer to his wife the same toward-her orientation, attributes, and actions he witnessed in God's relationship to him. These would lead to the blessing of God upon the relationship, the marriage's proper functioning, and the personal fulfillment of both individuals in the marriage.

From the beginning in Genesis, leadership is found in the heart of God and is given as a loving gift from our Creator to us. Leadership therefore is an opportunity to *bear the image of God* in relationship to one another. It is inextricably tied to godliness. Instead of merely allowing leadership as an unavoidable evil, God intended the world to function according to its dynamic. When fulfilled in a way consistent with his design, leadership is a beautiful, godly, and effective component of living that blesses human relationships and institutions, supplies security and function to the social order, contributes to the achievement of God's purposes, and brings great glory to God.

Leadership is an opportunity to bear the image of God in relationship to one another. It is inextricably tied to godliness.

Leadership in the Bible

After the fall, leadership—just like everything else in the world—was stained with sin. Though the world changed, the heart of God for his creation, his acts of influence toward that creation, and his implanting of leadership into the social order continued. Two types of leadership emerge in the biblical accounts: positional and personal.

Positional Leadership. In the Old Testament, the most basic form of leadership was expressed through the established power and authority attendant with official positions, titles, and roles. God established an order for the proper functioning of his people, and roles of leadership were at the heart of that order. From the smallest social unit to the largest, God ordained positions of authority, and when people in those positions acted in godly and responsible ways, the Lord's blessing was upon them and those under them.

In the family unit, husbands were established to lead their wives, and mothers and fathers were to lead their children. Beyond the family, leaders were appointed to act as local judges in the community

(Exodus 18) and oversee regional tribes (Numbers 1:1–19). National leaders also arose. Moses became leader of the Jewish nation by the calling of God. Joshua succeeded him and led Israel into the Promised Land.

As the early history of Israel unfolded, God established the leadership role of the prophet. These leaders possessed spiritual authority, often speaking on behalf of God to existing rulers as well as to the people of the nation. They were used by God to instruct, warn, and correct others in his ways (e.g., Samuel, Elijah, and Elisha). Following the conquest of the Promised Land, judges directed the affairs of the loose confederation of the tribes of Israel. They ruled, provided military leadership, and presided over legal disputes.

After the mostly damaging experience of the judges of Israel, the elders pleaded for a king to lead the nation. Although their request was displeasing to God, under his grace and sovereignty the Lord permitted the monarchy to be established, and he directed the prophet Samuel to appoint a king. The kingdom was divided after the reigns of Saul, David, and Solomon, and eventually the monarchies of Israel and Judah ended. God's people were now conquered, dispersed, and in exile under pagan domination. The Old Testament would close with a period characterized by prophets who exercised spiritual leadership while in exile. People such as Amos, Hosea, Isaiah, Micah, Nahum, Zephaniah, and Jeremiah were established by God to yield some form of influence over a diminishing remnant of Jews, speak God's truth to pagan power, and foretell impending judgment.

The great volume of leadership in the Old Testament is characterized as positional, that is, having the right to exercise leadership over others because of authoritative title, role, or function.

Likewise, the New Testament speaks of positional leadership. Though the roles and offices change, we still see God-ordained positions of leadership for the sake of the proper functioning of the church. These include apostles, prophets, evangelists, pastors, elders, teachers, overseers, and deacons (Ephesians 4:11, 1 Peter 5:1–5, 1 Timothy 3:1–10). Similarly, political governing authorities seem to be commissioned under God's sovereignty to bless, protect, and provide for the social order (Romans 13:1-7).

Positional leadership means the ability to exercise leadership over others due to authoritative title, role, or function.

Personal Leadership. Though positional leadership is prominent in Scripture, the Bible both instructs and implies a higher form of influence that is more consistent with the heart of God as ultimately expressed in his Son. This is leadership not related solely to the *position* of the leader, but to the *person* of the leader. This "more excellent way" yields influence through the power of love (1 Corinthians 12:31). It flows from the character of the person leading and the qualities he or she expresses that build trust, credibility, and inspiration within followers. In fact, the Scripture intimates that even those with positional power should manifest a higher form of influence that goes beyond position and title—one that is uniquely Christian, that acts in the best interest of those being led, and that is rooted in the morality and motivations of the leader. (Genesis 50; 1 Kings 3:9, 12:1-19; Psalm 78:70-72; John 13:12-15; Acts 20:28; Romans 13:1-4; 1 Peter 5:1-3)

Positional Leadership	Personal Leadership
Leads through power and authority	Leads through love, sacrifice, and service
Exhibits command and control	Exhibits empowerment & encouragement
Possesses the right to lead through title	Earns the right to lead through trust
Key Actions: Rules and Regulates	Key Actions: Influences and Inspires

There may be no more powerful, practical example of this difference than Paul's leadership toward the church in Thessalonica. In chapter 2 of 1 Thessalonians, Paul states that he sought to express the higher form of personal leadership *rather than* positional leadership, even though he possessed the latter: "Nor did we seek glory from men, either from you or from others, even though as apostles of Christ we might have asserted our authority" (1 Thessalonians 2:6, NASB). He states that in contrast to authoritative rule, he loved the Thessalonians and became among them as a nursing mother (2:7); a faithful, hard worker (2:9); and a loving father who would "exhort, encourage, and implore" his children (2:11). These influencing verbs are very different from the "command and control" kind of leadership that often typifies the positional approach.

People tend to respond to positional leadership mostly due to fear. The leader in position over a follower may reward one who responds appropriately or punish one who does not. While positional leadership might bring someone into submission and conformity, lasting impact and influence tends to come from personal leadership. Positional leadership alters one's external behavior and is therefore often only temporary in its influence. Personal leadership has the potential to transform the heart and mind and can lead to lasting impact.

I am a father of three. My initial leadership to my children is based upon the title and the authority vested in my role as father. In this sense, I might be able to get them to conform to my expectations simply because I hold an authoritative position over them. But if my children only do what I tell them to do because I hold the title of father, then I have failed as a parent. That kind of leadership will only last until they leave our home. While I do hold the title of leader, I will not have fulfilled the wonderful blessing and opportunity of the role as God designed it. If I seek lasting impact, I must instead *influence* my children through character and example. I must live before them, with passion, the values I hold dear in the hopes that they will embrace them as well. I must not just teach them and tell them what to do, but serve and sacrifice for my children in order to earn real credibility. I must provide a vision for them of the kind of life I desire them to live, as well as empower them with the potential to live it. This is the virtue of love inherent in biblical leadership, and it represents God's ultimate intent for believers who lead others.

Paul exemplified and Jesus epitomized true, biblical leadership when personal leadership is expressed through positional leadership (1 Thessalonians 2, Philippians 2:5–11)—that is, when leaders who hold position and power use that position and power for the benefit of others. Said another way, *when people who possess the right to lead through title also earn the right to lead through trust, then leadership as God intends is expressed.* Here, the magnanimity of leadership as designed by God is unveiled.

Personal leadership means the credibility to exercise leadership toward others due to the character and actions of the leader, which build trust and inspiration within followers.

Leaders in the Bible

From the Bible's perspective, leadership involves any task, role, or office to which God calls a man or woman that achieves God's purposes and impacts his people for his glory. Any person in the Bible who fits within this description is a candidate for the label *leader.*

Throughout Scripture, God deployed many men and women in this fashion. People such as Adam, Noah, Abraham, Joseph, Moses, Deborah, Nehemiah, Esther, Isaiah, Jonah, Paul, Timothy, Peter—all were led by God to achieve things that would bring him glory and achieve his purposes. Big or small, their God-given assignments realized particular and local objectives that blessed God's people and glorified the Father. These achievements were also a part of God's metanarrative. When combined, the individual successes of these leaders would prove integral to the overarching purposes of God in human history.

The Bible offers wonderful, insightful principles of effective leadership from these biblical characters and their experiences. For example, with Abraham we learn about the faith walk that always accompanies the call to biblical leadership; with Moses we learn about the importance of identity and its development in the heart of a leader; with Esther we learn of courage to lead despite great risk; with Nehemiah we gain insights into managing projects and people; with David we see the life and power available for leaders who develop intimacy with God, as well as the forgiveness available for them when great moral failure occurs; with Jeremiah we are inspired to endure and remain faithful to the call of God regardless of the circumstances surrounding that call; and with Paul we witness the credibility and trust gained through hard work and spiritual passion. Lessons such as these are many, are profound, and are included throughout the Bible to teach us about this thing called leadership.

Of value to this initial discussion are the patterns and principles that develop across all leaders of the Bible in their stories and in God's interaction with them. These are at the heart of what we might call a theology of leadership, and they begin to form a foundation for a definition of biblical leadership.

Toward a Theology of Leadership

1. Biblical leadership is comprehensive and diverse.

Leadership as seen from the Bible's perspective is not one-dimensional. It is not only about what leaders do. Rather, leadership is a multifaceted, holistic phenomenon in the Scripture, and it must be approached comprehensively. For example, the leadership experiences of Abraham, Joseph, Moses, Joshua, David, Esther, Nehemiah, Jeremiah, Daniel, Paul, and Peter were not only about the leadership task to which they were called. They also included:

- Person and personality—the leader's identity and character (see Genesis 17:5).
- Faith—God's purpose in calling the leader; the process of inner development; God's supernatural provision; and the faith in God that is required for the achievement of the leadership task (Genesis 22:1–19, Nehemiah 1–3, Daniel 1–3, Acts 16:25–30). In the Bible, the leader's faith and dependence upon God is a major subject inextricably planted into the leadership narrative (Hebrews 11:1–40). We often focus on the task achieved by the leader. *The Bible's focus is on the faith it took to achieve it.*
- The needs of God's people—what God sought to do in and for his people through this particular leader (Acts 16:6–10).
- The situation—the unique context to which God called the leader; the setting and context surrounding the leadership call (Exodus 3:1–20).

The faith of the leader is just as important as the achievement
of the task to which he or she is called.

---

2. Biblical leadership is moral.

The world might explain leadership merely in terms of influence: that is, a leader is someone who has the ability to affect the beliefs and behaviors of others (see chapter 2, "Contemporary Definitions"). But this limited definition would brand even people such as Hitler, Mussolini, and Charles Manson as effective leaders. After all, they had tremendous influence upon others.

The Bible offers a deeper perspective, one that is sorely needed in our world today. Throughout the leadership process—all the way from calling to completion—biblical leadership includes a moral component (see Psalm 78:72, 1 Timothy 3:1–13; 1 Peter 5:1–4). The God who calls the leader is moral; the leader must act in moral character; the means by which leaders influence others must be moral; the outcome of any leadership task should be moral and God-honoring in nature. Any part of this process that is immoral is one that defies leadership as explained in the Scripture.

3. Biblical leadership is God-oriented and people-focused.

The Bible reflects an ontological approach to leadership greatly missing in our world today. In our culture, leaders lead primarily to gain outcomes: numbers, profits, and a larger organization. This quantitative orientation creates many paradigms about leadership that are harmful in practice (these will be discussed later in the book). Leaders in the Bible, by contrast, were primarily concerned with obedience to God as opposed to outcomes and results. Effective leadership, according to the Bible, should always be measured first in terms of faithfulness to what God wants and then in terms of what it seeks to accomplish in and for *people* to the glory of God.

This goes beyond mere quantitative results. Rather, the Bible concerns itself *primarily* with qualitative outcomes (e.g. making disciples, loving one another, serving from the heart), and these are always related to God's intentions for his people. How are God's people transformed as a result of the leader's presence and his or her acts of leadership? The outcome of biblical leadership always yields some benefit to that which matters immensely to God—namely, people.

(For more on this, see Genesis 12:1–3; Joshua 1:6; Esther 4:13–17; Nehemiah 1:1–11; Hosea 2:14–23; Jonah 3:1–10; Isaiah 42:1–4; Matthew 9:11–13, 35–37, 28:18–21; Galatians 1:15–16; Philippians 3:13–21.)

4. Biblical leadership concerns the leader's character and motivation.

Often, God's call to a leadership task unveils the strength of the leader's character—or the lack thereof. Almost as important as the task itself is what God seeks to do in the person leading. In fact, in the Bible God's internal development of a leader in terms of faith and character occurs concurrent with the achievement of the leadership task. Wherever the Bible describes leaders and leadership situations, the faith, character, and motivations of the one leading becomes a major topic of the narrative (1 Samuel 16:7, Psalm 19:13–14, Psalm 78:72, Proverbs 17:2–3, Proverbs 21:2, Matthew 23:26–28, Acts 20:32–35, 1 Thessalonians 2:4). As God seeks to do a work *through* the leader, God does a work *within* the leader. This inner work, and how it applies to leaders today, must be studied as well.

5. Biblical leadership is fueled by and honors God.

The call to biblical leadership always includes a call for dependence upon the Father. It's not just that God wants us to do something. He wants us to be vessels by which *he* will do something. Leaders often miss this. They set out to do things *for* God. Rather, it is God who seeks to do things *through* them. Therefore, faith and constant dependence upon God are at the heart of what it means to be a biblical leader. In the end, when a leader depends upon God for both the internal and external resources necessary to achieve the leadership task, it is God who gets the credit and glory (Hebrews 11:1–40).

Leaders often set out to do things for God. Rather,
it is God who seeks to do things through them.

Chapter Review Questions

1. Why is the study of leadership important in the preparation of students for ministry?
2. Explain how Jesus was more than a teacher conveying a message.
3. What are some attributes of God that help us understand what leaders should be and do?

4. In what ways did God include leadership in the social functioning of the world?
5. List some differences between positional leadership and personal leadership.
6. What is a leader from the Bible's perspective?
7. What does it mean to say that "biblical leadership is comprehensive"?
8. Is leadership more than simple influence? Why?
9. What is always the object of true, biblical leadership?
10. Explain the difference between leaders who go out to do something for God and leaders who seek to be vessels by which God can do something. If we as leaders seek to be vessels through which God works, then what are the things we should primarily focus upon?

CHAPTER 2

WHAT IS BIBLICAL LEADERSHIP?

"Just about every popular notion about leadership is a myth."
JAMES M. KOUZES AND BARRY Z. POSNER

In one of the first leadership classes I taught, I asked my class, "What is a leader?" After an awkward silence, one of the students said, "I can't define what a leader is, but I know one when I see one."

While not the most comprehensive answer, this student's response is quite common. Most people cannot define the word *leader*, but they have an innate sense about leadership and have lived through experiences that help them recognize a good leader from a poor one. Thomas Cronin may have said it best: "Leadership is hard to define and even harder to quantify because it is part purpose, part process, and part product; part the why and part the how; part the artistic and intuitive, and only part the managerial."[9]

The reason for people's intuitive perceptions about leaders and leadership is that leaders have always existed in our world. From the earliest days until now, leaders have emerged from every social strata, civilization, and sphere of life. Individuals, groups, organizations, and even entire nations have felt their impact. The phenomenon of one individual's ability to influence another, through some means and for some purpose, is a natural part of our existence, and it permeates the very fabric of the human social order as designed by God.

Despite these experiences and perceptions, much is still misunderstood about leadership. This chapter will explore a brief history of academic leadership theories over the past sixty years, including contemporary definitions by popular authors. Finally, these theories and definitions will be contrasted with biblical notions of leadership—defining and displaying the uniqueness of leadership as explained in the Bible.

Academic Theories of Leadership

Throughout history, humans have attempted to comprehend the phenomenon of leadership. Confucius sought laws of order between leaders and subordinates. Plato described an ideal republic, with philosopher-kings providing wise and judicious leadership. The leadership exploits of kings, conquerors, and religious and political figures have been written about for centuries. It seems that God created the world to function according to the dynamic of leadership and endowed humans with an innate desire to understand it. Today, there are now literally hundreds of leadership development course programs at American postsecondary institutions.

Modern conceptions of leadership began as an aftereffect of the industrial revolution and were formed from the notion of "management," which itself grew from the need for efficiency in factory workers in the early twentieth century. Frederick Taylor, known as the Father of Scientific

Management, introduced the concepts of mechanization, specialization, and bureaucracy into the workplace. Under Taylor's influence, workers were likened to machines, efficiency in production was the primary measure of success, and managers were the "thinkers and leaders" in the organization.

The formal study of leadership arose primarily in the United States, and almost exclusively after the turn of the twentieth century.

In the 1950s, concurrent with the rise of the scientific method, empirical research on leadership began, and a multitude of ideas and methodologies to explain the phenomenon resulted. Over the past sixty years, leadership research gave birth to five major strains of leadership theory. Today, almost all secular, scholarly notions about the subject can be categorized into these five groups.

One of the earliest notions about leadership was Trait Theory. Trait Theory asserted that certain personal qualities—traits—were necessary for effective leadership and that people were either born with these traits or not. In the 1950s, researcher Ralph Stogdill outlined the particular traits associated with leadership, including such things as assertiveness, confidence, decisiveness, persistence, and ambition. Additionally, certain skills such as persuasiveness, fluent speech, and diplomacy were assigned. But the theory weakened as it failed to define with certainty what traits to include or exclude.

The Behavioral Approach became the dominant way of explaining leadership in the late 1950s and early 1960s. Different patterns of behavior were grouped together and labeled as "styles." Training in leadership styles became a very popular activity within management—perhaps the best known model being Blake and Mouton's Managerial Grid (1964). The grid plots the degree of task-centeredness versus person-centeredness and identifies five combinations as distinct leadership styles. The goal was for leaders to identify their inherent style and then develop in the leadership skills they lacked. However, as with Trait Theory, there was no agreement upon which behaviors were essential for effective leadership, and multiple exceptions undermined the theory's application.

Social Theory suggests that leadership is a process by which individuals and groups work toward the common goal of improving quality of life for all. The motivation for this work comes from social exchanges between leader and follower. It was originally conceived as LMX (Leader-Member Exchange) Theory (Graen, 1975). Prior to this work, leadership was seen as something that leaders did to their followers. LMX Theory asserted that leaders of groups maintain their position of influence through a series of tacit exchange agreements with group members. Leadership here is about meeting social needs and making mutually beneficial exchanges. Transactional Leadership Theory (Bass, 1981) falls under this category as well. In transactional leadership, leaders provide reward or recognition in exchange for follower loyalty and productivity. The leader motivates and directs followers primarily by appealing to their own self-interest.

Contingency Theory assumes that follower performance depends on leadership style as well as the favorableness of the leadership situation toward that style. Fiedler (1951) first described the theory in terms of motivation toward achieving tasks or building relationships, as well as the situational favorableness for either motivation. Situational favorableness was determined by three factors: (a) leader-member relations—the degree to which a leader is accepted and supported by the group members; (b) task structure—the extent to which the task is structured and defined, with clear goals and procedures; and (c) position power—the ability of a leader to control subordinates through reward and punishment. Fiedler suggested that it may be easier for leaders to change their situation to achieve effectiveness rather than to change their leadership style.

Consistent with this notion of contingency, Hersey and Blanchard's Situational Leadership model suggests there is no one best way to influence people (1977). Here, the leadership style one should use depends on the readiness level of the people the one is attempting to influence. Situational leadership is based on the interplay among (1) the amount of guidance and direction (directive behavior) a leader gives, (2) the amount of socio-emotional support (supportive behavior) a leader provides, and (3) the developmental level that followers exhibit in commitment and competence in order to perform a specific task, function, or objective. This model has been slightly revised by Blanchard (Situational Leadership II) and is widely used today in employee and management training in America.

But the most prominent and studied leadership theory over the past twenty years is the model of Transformational Leadership. James MacGregor Burns first theorized about and described a transformational approach to leadership in 1978. Later, Bass (1990) expanded this theory and categorized the activity of the transformational leader. He outlined four behaviors that represent effectiveness in leadership as these behaviors "transform" followers: (a) individualized consideration, (b) intellectual stimulation, (c) inspirational motivation, and (d) idealized influence. Peter G. Northouse (2004) states that transformational leadership refers to the process "whereby an individual engages with others and creates a connection that raises the level of motivation and morality in both the leader and the follower."[10] Most concur that transformational leadership takes place over time as leaders develop "trust, admiration, loyalty and respect."[11]

Finally, more recent and postmodern approaches to understanding leadership have been expressed. Theories such as Chaos Theory and Complexity Theory state that effective leaders should be comfortable with uncertainty and ambiguity, resist linear systems of thinking, defy rationalistic forms of decision making, and learn the art of leading without a rigid future orientation. Beyond traditional skills and behaviors, leaders should have "emotional intelligence" (Goleman, 2005), embrace postmodern needs for authenticity and community, and understand that contemporary motivations for work and productivity go beyond making money into finding life meaning. While novel and interesting, postmodern theories remain essentially consistent with previous notions in regard to demands for particular leader behavior.

Outline of Major Academic Theories

THEORY	ASSERTION
Trait Theory	All leaders must possess certain competencies and traits
Behavioral Theory	Leaders must learn behaviors common to good leadership
Social Theory	Effectiveness is found in leader practices that allow social exchanges between leader and follower
Contingency Theory	Leadership styles (sets of behaviors) must match certain leadership contexts and situations
Transformational Theory	Leaders should express behaviors that inspire and transform followers
Postmodern Theories	Leaders must learn to adjust to complexity and respond with skills that are effective in a postmodern context

Remarkably, with all the topic's history and extensive research, there remains today no single, unifying definition of leadership, and researchers are still at odds as to how to approach its study. It seems that leadership remains "one of the most observed and least understood phenomena on earth."[12]

Contemporary Definitions

Resulting from the above academic theories and the assumptions behind them, an amazing number of popular-press articles, periodicals, and books exist about the subject of leadership—most of which have come from the business sector in America. The authors, often celebrated as leadership "gurus," are greatly admired; and their books, conferences, and consulting services have become a multibillion-dollar industry.

There remains today no single, unifying definition of leadership.

In their book *Leaders: The Strategies for Taking Charge,* Warren Bennis and Burt Nanus state, "Decades of academic analysis has given us more than 850 definitions of leadership."[13] Noticeably, most of them are not biblical in that they do not flow from the Bible or from any suitable theological framework. Additionally, there is a difference between definitions that merely do not conflict with God's Word and those that flow directly from it—that is, a lack of conflict does not make a definition "biblical."

Many Christian authors and scholars approach the biblical case for leadership in the following way. They look at "effective" leaders and their functioning in the world and generate definitions of leadership based upon what they observe. Then, they find Bible verses that might match and support their observations. This inductive, back-ended way into truth is filled with pitfalls. In the end, they may even end up undergirding very nonbiblical assumptions with the Bible. For those who desire to build a biblical theology of leadership, of first importance is the question, what does the Bible disclose about who a leader is and what he or she does?

A summary of definitions of leadership by contemporary authors reveals some amazing insights into current cultural paradigms about the concept:

Peter Drucker states, "Leadership is defined by results not attributes."[14]

John Maxwell says, "The true measure of leadership is influence—nothing more, nothing less."[15]

Gary Yukl defines leadership as "the process of influencing others to understand and agree about what needs to be done and how to do it, and the process of facilitating individual and collective efforts to accomplish shared objectives."[16]

Peter Northouse defines leadership as "a process whereby an individual influences a group of individuals to achieve a common goal."[17]

Ken Blanchard defines leadership as "the capacity to influence others by unleashing the potential and power of people and organizations for the greater good."[18]

James M. Kouzes and Barry Z. Posner, in their seminal book *The Leadership Challenge* (1987), state that five practices define effective leadership:

- Model the way. Leaders lead first by example, incorporating into their own lives the beliefs and behaviors they demand of their followers.
- Inspire a shared vision. Leaders envision the future, creating an ideal and unique image of what the organization can become.
- Challenge the process. Leaders search for opportunities to change the status quo and innovative ways to improve the organization.
- Enable others to act. Leaders foster collaboration and build spirited teams. They actively involve others.
- Encourage the heart. Leaders recognize contributions that individuals make and share in the rewards of achievements.[19]

Noted author and consultant Steven Covey states, "My definition of leadership is communicating to people their worth and potential so clearly that they are inspired to see it in themselves."[20]

While these observations may be salient, they fall short of giving a view of leadership that is based in the Bible and the character of God.

The Missing Eggs

When my daughter Kaley was young, we enjoyed baking together. We would listen to music and sing while mixing batter and then enjoy our yummy creation fresh out of the oven. One day we decided to bake a cake. Using a store-bought cake mix, we gathered the ingredients needed and combined them all in a bowl, put the mix in a pan, and placed it in the oven. When the timer went off, we retrieved the cake. To our surprise, it didn't look much like a cake. Rather, it looked much more like a thick, brown tortilla! After some discussion, we realized that we had forgotten to put eggs into the mix. What we ended up with was not quite a cake. Apparently, what ruined the cake was not the ingredients we included— those were essential to its creation. Rather, the flawed cake resulted from *what we left out.*

The theories and definitions discussed in this chapter have added beneficial insights to our understanding of the dynamic of leadership. Many of the ideas are in fact vital to comprehending the phenomenon of one person's influence upon another. But just as with our flawed cake, the problems we witness in leadership today, both in theory and practice, do not result from what's been included in the discussion. Rather, they flow from what's been left out. With respect to leadership, *the cake is missing the eggs.* Even with all the theories and definitions, we are left with "not quite a leader" when compared to the Bible's characterizations.

The primary reason for this insufficiency has already been discussed: these theories and definitions almost exclusively focus on *what leaders do*—that is, they concentrate on the external skills, behaviors, and practices of leaders. The Bible portrays a much different picture. In the Scripture, leadership is not primarily about what leaders do. Rather, it is first a function of *who leaders are.* This includes not only the behaviors of leaders, but also their character, their faith in God, their motivating purpose, and God's supernatural work in and through them. These ingredients are in fact the missing eggs.

This singular focus upon the external and perceptible as found among leadership theories and popular definitions has created assumptions that lead to the downfall of the practice of leadership in our world today.

Duplicitous Leaders

Since external behavior has supplanted most talk of motivations and inner character when it comes to leadership, leaders have learned to become bifurcated. The practices of the leader are believed to be separate and distinct from his or her character and motivations. Character is separated from conduct. So students of leadership concern themselves with learning external skills without understanding the dire need for the character that brings life, authenticity, and security to those skills. As a result, those in leadership give more emphasis to appearance and style—how others perceive them—rather than to who they actually are.

Coming from that perspective, leadership is reduced to a cosmetic of sorts:—something one paints on the outside that is detached from who one is. At a deeper level, this external focus produces a paradigm of duplicity in the leader, a subconscious idea that leadership is only about public persona. Duplicitous leaders are those with two lives—one public and one private—as well as the belief that one does not impact the other. This assumption results in double-minded leaders who lead from image, plausibility, and spin rather than from an authentic expression of who they are. Believing that they must always "do before others" what will gain results and approval, such leaders become distinct in their public image from who they are in reality. Leadership is simply a façade.

Sadly, this squelches the unique way God could work in an individual and creates deep insecurity within the leader who must act the part.

Duplicitous leaders are those with two lives—a
public one and a private one—
thinking that one does not impact the other.

Cult of Personality

Since the prevailing assumption is that leadership is external, not only do potential leaders focus solely on the superficial, but followers do as well.

Consequently, there is an unhealthy addiction among people to placing leaders on pedestals, judging them by superficial standards, and being swept away by dynamic personalities.

When this occurs, leaders become more than change agents: they become the reason for change themselves. Followers respond to the leader's personal charm or surface-level skill and charisma. The result is an idealized and heroic public image, often built up through unquestioned flattery and praise.

Many churches today are built solely upon the powerful, dynamic personalities of their leaders. Tragically, the persona of the leader becomes the focus rather than the vision of God for the church.

This is not to say that we should dismiss energetic and animated personalities. God uses all unique expressions of personality or gifting to reveal his vision and lead his people. But the great temptations for these leaders include the abuse of power, a blind and subconscious hypocrisy, and a susceptibility to accepting the praises of men that are due only to Christ.

Consequentialism

Today's definitions and theories about leadership hold yet another major flaw. They all measure leader effectiveness almost exclusively in quantitative terms: profits, number of followers, and/or size of the organization. As it stands, many churches and corporations call a leader successful if he or she achieves this kind of success—the exact definition of which no one can agree upon. How many followers must one have in order to be a "great leader"? Is it five, ten, a majority . . . all of them? How much profit? How big an organization?

Consequentialism is the philosophical and ethical premise that says the results of one's conduct are the true basis for any judgment about the morality of that conduct. "Rightness" is not inherently attached to an action or the motivation for that action, but rather to the *consequence* of that action. For example, consequentialism would argue that speaking the truth could indeed be wrong if the consequences of doing so were harmful. Alternatively, lying could be right if it produces benefit to the leader. In consequentialism, an act (or omission of an act) is moral if it yields a good outcome, regardless of the means or the motivations that produced that act. Consequentialism is closely associated with *pragmatism*—yet another errant prevailing philosophy that produces errant practices of leadership. Whereas consequentialism says "The ends justify the means," pragmatism says, "If it works, do it."

Consequentialism defines "rightness"
by results, not by the morality
of the act itself or the motivations behind it.

Because of the underlying assumption of consequentialism, leaders today focus on getting quantitative results at all expense. This is the driving force for them—the need for more, bigger, and better. Leaders then judge themselves and others based upon these superficial standards. But is such a morally relativistic approach really of God?

In Christian leadership, these utilitarian paradigms often lead to a focus with several misguided applications:

- What works as opposed to what's right
- Numeric growth as opposed to spiritual health
- An obsession with the fruit of ministry rather than the faithfulness of the minister
- The end product as opposed to the moral process
- Obtaining a following as opposed to remaining obedient to God
- Attracting church attenders instead of developing disciples of Jesus

Christian leaders must think deeply and critically about what it means to be an effective leader. Is it biblical for us to measure leadership solely in terms of number of followers?

For example, in John 6, when Jesus teaches that he is the Bread of Life, the apostle John explains that this was a difficult notion for his followers to accept. John states, "From this time many of his disciples turned back and no longer followed him" (John 6:66). If Jesus's leadership were assessed at this point in his ministry by today's consequentialist standards, would he be labeled an ineffective leader? What about at his crucifixion, when all deserted him? Most church growth conferences would not highlight such a strategy! Was Jeremiah an ineffective leader because people did not respond to his message?

We can cite many other examples of those from the Bible we deem great leaders, yet whose followers did not respond in the moment to their leadership. Does true leadership, as defined biblically, mean quantity of followers or *quality* of followers—or at times even a total lack of followers? Beyond practical skills, is true leadership based also upon a set of ontological values to which leaders must remain true regardless of the following they gain or lose? These are questions with which the student of biblical leadership must wrestle.

Methodolatry

Since "whatever works is right" is a core assumption of our secular leadership culture, many leaders naturally focus on programs and methods that are deemed effective in gaining a following. This mind-set is also prevalent in the church.

Let's say Pastor Jake is a struggling leader who attends a church growth conference. One night he hears from a pastor who leads a large, fast-growing church. This church approaches ministry a certain way—by employing certain programs and methods—and the large-church pastor possesses a certain style and personality. Pastor Jake determines that what his church needs is a different approach. He concludes that he should display a different persona, and that his church must change its methods (music, attire, ministry programs, teaching style, etc.). He goes back to the congregation and immediately begins implementing new ways of doing things—possibly to the long-term detriment of his church.

This experience, repeated time and again in ministry, is a textbook example not only of how *not* to implement change, but also of a pervasive paradigm present in church leaders today. The assumption is that what works in one church ministry will obviously work in another.

Leading change that comes from God's vision is one thing, and it is always right to do. But when the way we do church is elevated above God's supernatural work in the church, we've committed *methodolatry*. We've come to worship the method above the God who worked in and through the method. Programs, methods, and ministries learned from other churches and leaders are not inherently wrong to apply, but they should be birthed by God through the unique vision of a particular congregation. A.W. Tozer said, "Heresy of method may be as deadly as heresy of message"[21] and what often undermines borrowed methods is that God has been left out.

Methodolatry minimizes God's role and supernatural activity
and instead focuses on the way in which he worked.
The object of trust becomes the method rather than God.

I would argue, in fact, that the process that gives birth to a particular ministry or method is *more* important than the method itself. Why? Because it is in that process where God's people interact with the Father and usher in faith to trust him for some expression of his manifest will. The process also validates the method in the hearts and minds of people, thereby making it authentic and organic for them. It is what builds faith in God and fuels the actual ministry once it's implemented.

When people believe that God has led them to do something, then the values associated with the method are present in them, and those values will sustain any change related to the method once implemented. We certainly don't always have to be original in our methods, but we should always be authentic.

Methodolatry has four tragic results. First, it minimizes God's role in the work of the originating church, highlighting the method and the church rather than the God who worked through it.

Second, it causes pastors not to be true to themselves and instead to seek to become someone or something they're not. The heartbreaking, unspoken assumption is that I must be someone else in order for God to use me. Trying to be someone else is a waste of the person God made *you* to be.

Third, it preempts God's ability to work in unique ways through a distinct church family and their story of faith.

And fourth, the object of trust becomes the method itself rather than God.

Leaders don't always have to be original in their methods,
but they should always be authentic.

The Subtle Drift

Possibly the saddest occurrence coinciding with the rise of the study of leadership in the twentieth century was the drift of God's people away from the Bible as the standard of truth. The church, like the world, bought into the "whatever works" paradigm. Thus, the widespread, secular assumptions in both the academic theories and popular literature of leadership became pervasive and difficult for God's people to withstand. This eventually led to the people of God accepting the wholesale assumptions of worldly leadership, and the church began to take its leadership cues from a secular culture.

This is an ongoing problem today. The business sector in particular is celebrated as the ultimate source of truth about leadership—as opposed to God's Word.

The trouble is, we are borrowing concepts from an upside-down world. Since what was practiced in business seemed to work, the church coopted leadership principles from corporate America. The evangelical church in particular began to believe that businesspeople did it better. Those in the church who possessed great business acumen (but who possibly had very little understanding of what God intended for the church) populated church boards. Churches became corporations. Pastors became CEOs. Christian authors borrowed rather worldly concepts, slapped a Scripture verse or two on them, and called it "Christian leadership"—when in actuality they were promoting fleshly principles cloaked in spiritual language. This left the church with little distinction in our culture, an anemic entity copying the world, having little impact, and struggling at best to survive.

Yet, in this context God has provided a vast mission field of opportunity. Biblical leadership is needed now more than ever. As believers, we have a unique and wonderful calling to address the leadership crisis—and we have solid ground on which to stand. If we will recommit ourselves to the standard of God's Word as opposed to taking our beliefs from the culture, we may catch a glimpse of the brilliant possibilities for biblical leadership and the stark, colorful difference this kind of leadership will make in the middle of a world full of shades of gray.

Distinctives of Biblical Leadership

Biblical leadership involves several distinctives that set it in sharp contrast to the leadership theories and definitions of the modern world.

Character. Character is that set of moral qualities that distinguishes one person from others. These qualities include things such as honesty, courage, integrity, humility, perseverance, and decisiveness. Yet it's important to understand that these traits do not just happen. They actually flow from a deeper structure within the individual. In order to be authentic, these qualities must be connected to a person's identity—i.e., how that person sees and defines him or herself. As the Scripture says, it is from the heart of a person that proper attitudes and actions flow (Proverbs 4:23).

Character not only includes the moral traits of an individual, but the very inner structure of the individual from which those traits flow.

But this identity or sense of self should not be the result of our own invention. It's not ultimately important who we say we are, nor is it important who others say we are. What is vitally important is who God says we are. This is true especially for leaders, because in time, our true selves will show through to those we lead.

In the life of Jesus, we see ways he viewed and defined himself that have particular relevance to leadership. As leaders seeking to practice biblical leadership, we must also desire to assimilate his character and self-definition into our lives.

The character of the biblical leader may be summarized by three images directly connected to who Jesus was and how he led. These images are the ways that Jesus defined himself in his leadership (influence) toward others. They are the images of the *servant,* the *steward,* and the *shepherd.* These dimensions provide the Christian leader with metaphors by which to grasp the Bible's teaching about how leaders should see themselves. Leaders who seek to walk in integrity and assimilate Jesus's character into their being will more naturally express traits of moral character as well as be more naturally empowered to know what to do in practice as they go about leading others.

Additionally, we must be careful to apply these images to the idea of *character* first and not to *conduct*—lest we fall into the mind-set that so often typifies the world's approach— namely, that leadership is merely something we do on the outside. The Bible student will make a big error if he or she only seeks to *act* as a servant, a steward, and a shepherd without *becoming* those things—that is, without taking on the character of each. Can a person serve others without a servant's heart? Well, possibly and temporarily. But that equates to acting a part rather than developing a disposition of servanthood in their person. In time, without full integration and character development, the leader is not able to continue to prop up the character traits necessary for biblical leadership. They are simply too difficult to pretend.

Christlike character, then, is the first distinctive of biblical influence. This is true because it is the primary work of the Holy Spirit after salvation to build that character in the believer. Without it, leaders are merely empty shells, actors who play a part, void of substance and lasting spiritual impact. Leaders like this might impress people with their skills and thus gain a following. But they have the potential to enduringly transform others only through character.

When manifested, character creates the credibility for a leader to be respected and trusted and to earn the right to influence others. Biblical leaders commit themselves to the lifelong pursuit of assimilating the character of a servant, steward, and shepherd into their being.

Calling. Biblical leaders must not only concern themselves with how to lead, but they must also address *why* they are leading—for what purpose. Most authors use the term *vision* to describe a leader's purpose and the future state for which they influence others. While the idea of vision is at the heart of leading others, to comprehend biblical leadership we must realize that in a biblical paradigm, vision flows first from God's call to the leader.

Why is this an important distinction? Well, if we're not careful, vision will turn out to be something we *invent* rather than something we *discover* from God. The term "calling" possesses the inherent idea that purpose comes from God to us—not the other way around. With a calling, after all, there must be a Caller. (See Genesis 12:1–4, Exodus 3:1–6, 1 Samuel 16:12, Isaiah 6:1–13, Jeremiah 1:4–7, Mark 3:14–15, John 15:16, Acts 9:1–16, Romans 15:15–18).

Often, a leader's plans get confused with God's plan. We have a dream, an aspiration, or a goal, and it becomes what we believe is God's vision. We then go to God to convince him to get on board with what *we* want to see happen in the world. In essence we say, "God, please bless and resource MY plans." This leads to failure, frustration, and misguided achievements, since God did not author the vision in the first place. Here, leaders achieve only to realize the achievements were not of God. As Howard Hendricks profoundly said, "The fear is not for leaders to fail, but to succeed at doing the wrong thing."

The fact is, *God has not committed himself to finance our dreams.* He's not a genie in the bottle who exists to grant our wishes. He wants us to get involved in his plans. Calling therefore communicates something received from God (the One calling) to us (the ones called)—and God is always faithful to supply and sustain that which he initiates. The great promise to leaders who follow God's call is that he will be faithful to resource it.

God has not committed himself to finance our dreams.
We must adjust our lives to what he wants—
not seek to have him adjust to what we want.

Additionally, calling is an inherent biblical concept, as compared to the modern idea of "vision." The actual word *vision* in the Bible almost always refers to prophetic visions. This is different from the way vision is described in modern leadership. The term today, mostly used in business and corporate settings, blurs the lines between the purposes of a business and that of the church. Calling, on the other hand, is unique to people of faith. While vision (a mental idea of a preferable future) certainly flows from calling, leaders should first process and possess a strong sense of God's compelling call to join him in the work he is doing. After their response of faith to God's call, vision will begin to develop within the hearts and minds of the leaders—and most importantly, that vision will be rooted in a call from God, not in self-centered ambition.

Calling, therefore, is the force that drives and inspires biblical leaders to influence. It keeps them focused, provides accountability to act consistently, inspires them to endure hardships, and ensures that one's leadership results only in what God wants.

Competence. Psalm 78:72 states, "And David shepherded them with integrity of heart; with skillful hands he led them." Just as integrity of heart (i.e. character) is vital to biblical leadership, so are skillful hands (i.e. competence). Yet in the Scripture, skills are not mere cosmetics to be put on and taken off, nor are they disconnected from the leader's character. Rather, they are congruent complements to his or her inner person, and as such, they allow the leader to manifest God's calling in the world. Imagine Moses without the skill of delegating to others (Exodus 18:13–27), Nehemiah without the ability to manage projects and people (Nehemiah 4:13–23), or Paul without the skill of communicating spiritual truth to his readers (Colossians 1:28–29). These competencies provided for the success of their God-given callings and were used mightily by the Lord in their particular leadership contexts. In this sense, outer competence is related to inner character.

Not every leader has every skill. Students of leadership must come to understand both the skills common to effective, Christlike leadership and the skills unique to who they are. To do the former, students must discover from God's Word common competencies of effective leaders. To do the latter, one must give attention to discovering his or her spiritual gifts, natural competencies, unique personality, and God-given passions.

Community. While secular leaders might concern themselves with profits and material productivity, biblical leadership is seen in terms of impact upon and relationship to people. The idea of community applies in two ways.

First, the outcome of biblical leadership is always about transforming the lives of human beings. In the Scripture, every time God called a leader to a leadership task, God's purpose was to redeem and restore his people through the instrument of the leader. Therefore, biblical leadership does not ever exist in a vacuum. A biblical leader is an individual called of God to interact with and impact people. Biblical leadership is not primarily about developing a ministry program, sitting behind a computer, or constructing a building. It is not about profits, widgets, or organization size. Those may be a means toward a people-transforming end, but they are never the end in themselves—and if we are not careful, leaders can easily lose our way as to the real goal of leadership. People are of immense value to God, more important than anything numeric or material, and our leadership should have the development and transformation of people as its object.

The outcome of biblical leadership is
always about the transformation of human beings.
Always.

Second, biblical leadership takes place in the context of Christian community. Jesus didn't simply tell the disciples to show up at the temple once a week, and there he would lecture them on principles of leadership. Jesus did life with those he led. He chose to impart himself, not just his teaching. It was out of the context of that community between him and his disciples, with failures and victories alike, that they grew to achieve something of great value together.

Consequently, biblical leaders seek to develop open, authentic relationships with those they lead. Biblical leaders love the people they lead—they don't just use them. In the closest of relationships that a leader can possess with his or her followers, there is deep connection, vulnerability, understanding, and personal investment. Paul described his relationship to the Thessalonians just so: "Having so fond an affection for you, we were well-pleased to impart to you not only the gospel of God but also our own lives, because you had become very dear to us" (1 Thessalonians 2:8). Community breathes life into leadership and grounds it in the supreme moral virtue that must accompany all truly biblical leaders—namely, agape love.

Christ. Finally, worldly leaders may operate in their own strength and in their own wisdom, and they might be able to accomplish good and even noble things. But biblical leadership produces eternal results because it comes from a different source. It's not based upon the world's wisdom or the meager human resources of the leader. These sources can only accomplish what can be explained in natural and human ways and through the limited skills of the leader. By contrast, the inner fuel, guide, and force at work for the biblical leader is the very power of Christ.

Since this is so, biblical leadership must always be a walk of faith. Leadership acted upon with trust in God is then fueled by a supernatural force—Jesus himself! Christ accomplishes through the humble and obedient leader that which can only be ascribed to God's ability. In the end, the leader sees limitless possibilities for what can be achieved. Consequently, when the task is complete it is God, not the leader, who receives the credit.

Biblical leadership should always be a
walk of faith—asking God to do
beyond what the leader can do so that in
the end God receives the credit.

A Definition of Biblical Leadership

Biblical leadership is distinctly different from that described and defined by the world. The distinctives above help Christian leaders understand the unique way the Bible describes one person's influence upon another, the motivation behind that influence, the eventual outcome of that influence, and the source of power to guide and sustain that influence. This is biblical leadership!

> A *biblical leader is a person of* **character** *and* **competence** *who influences a* **community** *of people to achieve a God-honoring* **calling** *by means of the power of* **Christ***.*

Based upon this definition, this book will explore these five components of biblical leadership and the spheres of influence associated with each.

Character: the *person* of the leader.

Calling: the *purpose* of the leader.

Competence: the *practices* of the leader.

Community: the *people* of the leader.

Christ: the *power* of the leader.

Chapter Review Questions

1. List each category of academic theories of leadership since the 1950s and describe the core meaning of each.
2. How do leaders direct and motivate followers according to the Social Theory of leadership?
3. Name one of the academic theories of leadership that you agree with and why.
4. What is a characteristic of Transformational Leadership Theory that might intersect with the Bible's teaching about leadership? Explain what and how.
5. Why does Maxwell's definition of leadership, though helpful, fall short of what the Scripture teaches?
6. In what way is the "cake missing the eggs" as far as leadership theory and contemporary definitions are concerned?
7. List and briefly define each of the tragic results flowing from the world's assumptions about leadership.

8. List and explain the five distinctives of biblical leadership.
9. What are the three images of character as reflected in the leadership of Jesus?
10. What's the difference between *calling* and *vision*?
11. What difference does "Christ as the power of the leader" make?

CHAPTER 3

CHARACTER: THE PERSON OF THE LEADER

"The greatest crisis in the world today is a crisis of leadership, and the greatest crisis in leadership is a crisis of character."

HOWARD HENDRICKS

As a teacher on Christian leadership, I assign my students the task of creating a "life map" at the beginning of their course of study. It's an exercise where they honestly reflect upon their past and chart the defining experiences that have shaped who they are. It's a challenging assignment for most. The purpose is for students to become self-aware, to assign meaning to their former experiences, to understand the dynamics in their present life and leadership as a result, and to discover God's power to use all of life for good.

Upon completion, students share their life maps with the class. Out of the numerous life stories I have heard throughout the years, I would estimate that more than half of the students come from significantly broken or spiritually dysfunctional backgrounds . . . *and all of them are studying to become Christian leaders in organizations.*

This tragedy of brokenness is more than anecdotal. At no time in history has there been such an epidemic of personal instability and brokenness. Myriads of people are moving into adulthood with deep insecurities produced by a culture of divorce, addictive behavior, political unrest, sexual abuse, overstimulation, materialism, and spiritual dysfunction. Even those who grow up in wholeness and emotional health have no guarantees of well-being. The potent influences of our culture coupled with our own sinful nature develops in all of us harmful patterns of thinking, fleshly motivations, and distorted views of self.

As we will see, this background of brokenness is deeply pertinent to the discussion of biblical leadership.

The Character Crisis

One of the prevailing myths of our time is that these intrapersonal matters do not affect leaders in the function of leadership. Yet coinciding with the decay in our culture, we witness leader after leader flounder and fail. Immoral and unethical leadership has never been more prominent. Egocentric leaders are everywhere. Leaders driven by insecurity permeate almost every organization.

Of those who resist collapse, a large portion barely survive in leadership as they lack the inner resources necessary to endure the pressures of their roles, manage the power associated with them, bring about change, move people to accomplish purpose, and healthily influence others. It seems that the plethora of training workshops, books, and leadership conferences over the past sixty years have proven inadequate to halt the downward spiral.

While Scripture does not deny that certain competencies of leadership (what leaders do) are important, practical skills are only part of the leader equation. Many of us could cite leaders of great competence and skill, yet who lacked character. They were outstanding strategic thinkers, exceptional communicators, and possibly great motivators. Yet they lacked inner security; a firm identity in Christ; a growing, life-giving faith that resulted in a moral compass; and the ability to be authentic and vulnerable in their closest relationships. Consequently, secret sins developed, temptations associated with the power of leadership overwhelmed, and in time, these leaders succumbed to internal collapse. Almost inevitably they end up shipwrecking their marriages, families, churches, and organizations. They lacked the inner character to support the success created through their dynamic skill. In truth: *skills may take leaders where character won't keep them.*

The symptoms of this character crisis are many.

In leadership, skills may take you where character won't keep you.

Using Leadership to Meet Inner Needs

All of us as humans have a need for affirmation, love, and approval. All of us need to feel that we've achieved some measure of success. All of us need to believe that we are making a difference. These needs are a natural and innate part of our humanness. Yet, instead of meeting these needs through authentic connections to God and other people, there are those who illegitimately use leadership to fill their intrapersonal voids. In fact, I would say that many go into leadership not due to God's call or the healthy desire to serve others but to meet some inner need for significance, acceptance from others, or approval from God. There is something within them, something broken, something essentially about the self, that becomes medicated through leadership. Here, legitimate human needs are satiated through illegitimate means. This makes leadership something very dysfunctional in its practice, essentially more about the leader than about God's will or the people led.

Leadership is not a primary way to have needs met, be they needs for acceptance, achievement, or significance. In fact, if you try to meet needs this way, you'll be greatly disappointed. That's because leadership—*biblical* leadership—is more about imparting to others than receiving for self. It is more about others' needs than your own. Leadership takes more than it gives. Therefore, the person who uses leadership primarily as a way to get something deeply self-fulfilling sets him or herself up for disappointment.

Just like any other substitute for God, who alone can meet our deepest needs, leadership is insufficient *when used for a purpose it could never fulfill.*

Abusing Power and Position

Leaders who lack the inner security of character must manage their people and organizations in ways that advance their own agendas and personas. You see, what they want *must* occur. This motivation results in obsessive control, manipulating people and circumstances, the inability to admit wrong, the use of spin control when mistakes happen, making autonomous decisions, and the use of authority rather than godly influence to achieve one's way. Such leaders often lack the ability to let go, to learn from others, to listen, to share leadership, and to trust God with outcomes.

Denying, Deflecting or Defending Problems

Rather than take personal responsibility, leaders who lack character blame others or circumstances for problems, as well as hiding from elephant-in-the-room situations. When finally confronted, these leaders offer superficial fixes rather than deep, biblical solutions.

Leaders who lack character do not take responsibility.
Instead, they deny, deflect, and defend.

Misplaced Ideas of Success and Failure

I have a college friend who was in ministry along with me in those days. A few years ago I called him and asked him how his ministry was going. He said, "Mike, it's been very difficult, and for the past three years we've seen few results. But I've learned something very important. I've learned that God has not primarily called me to success. He has called me to obedience." Here is a leader who is experiencing the most secure form of joy in ministry—faithfulness to God.

Taking their cues from the culture, leaders void of character define success in superficial ways. A bigger church, more employees, greater material possessions, a larger salary, more notoriety—these are the symbols of success even for Christian leaders in the twenty-first century. Rather than defining success as faithfulness to God and simply expressing the person God created them to be, they measure success through worldly standards. Often cloaking their motivation in spiritual language and the expressed desire to achieve God's purposes, they are more accurately driven by selfish ambition.

Something to Prove

Leaders void of Christlike character subtly and subconsciously compare themselves and their organizations to others. They judge success by how well they do in contrast to others rather than by simple faithfulness to God. This leads to the experience of jealousy and insecurity when others apparently achieve more or to pride when they have surpassed their contemporaries in acquiring notable symbols of success.

Warren Bennis may have said it best:

No leader sets out to be a leader per se, but rather to express himself freely and fully. That is, leaders have no interest in proving themselves, but an abiding interest in expressing themselves. The difference is crucial, for it's the difference between being driven, as too many people are today, and leading, as too few people do.[22]

Low Emotional Capacity

All leaders feel stress at times, and the weight of leadership is often heavy. As Shakespeare said, "Uneasy lies the head that wears a crown".[23] Sometimes situations are so dysfunctional and support is so low that leaders should pray and consider leaving. Yet frequently, it is not the situation that needs changing. It is the leader.

Leaders without Christlike character will struggle to find the emotional resources required to meet the pressures of the job. Where inner security and identity in Christ are lacking, leaders become overwhelmed with the demands of the role, saying, "I just can't do this." They take critique very personally. They express escapist tendencies, including the constant need to get away (distancing themselves from the job as much as possible—this is in contrast to a legitimate need for occasional withdrawal in order to seek God and be restored), cowering away from feedback, isolating themselves from others, and a fear of trust and intimacy with those who could actually help them. Mostly, they feel they are victims and may even express martyr tendencies (blaming, manipulating others by guilt, feeling sorry for self, etc.). They struggle with overwhelming negative emotions such as sadness, anxiety, deep anger, and guilt. They may even grow depressed and physically fatigued.

Creating Insecure Organizations

Possibly the most tragic consequence of character-void leaders is the destructive impact they can have upon the people and organizations they lead. *Insecure people create environments of insecurity.*

> Leaders not only embed in their organizations what they intend consciously to get across, but they also convey their own inner conflicts and the inconsistencies in their own personal makeup.[24]

This dynamic is true whether it be in families, churches, or business organizations. Insecure leaders often fail to affirm and empower others. Or they fail to lead them due to fear. They often confuse people and create unsettled cultures in their organizations because people don't see consistency or logic in their actions. Insecure leaders are either quick to bring external change (jumping from one new fad to the next) or avoid change altogether when it threatens their leadership. They make illogical decisions not based upon what is best for the organization, but upon what validates them and affirms their leadership. This creates organizations that flounder internally in their functioning, externally in the achievement of a mission, or both.

Insecure, unhealthy leaders create insecure,
unhealthy organizations.

What Is Character?

It is only through the development of Christlike character that leaders may find hope and healing as well as the inner power to lead as the Bible instructs. But what is character according to the Bible?

In the Old Testament, the phrase translated "character" is *esheth chayil* (ליח תשא).[25] It includes the idea of power and strength that flows from within, and it may denote one who is virtuous. The accompanying adjective "noble" is used to convey the moral nature of the term in Ruth 3:11, Proverbs 12:4, and Proverbs 31:10.

In the New Testament, the most common Greek word for the concept is *dokime* (δοκιμη). The word study dictionary describes the word as in "proving, trial, approved, tried character; a proof, specimen of tried worth."[26] Strong's includes these definitions along with the idea of experience.[27]

The word or its derivatives is used seven times in six verses within the New Testament and is translated by the NASB as *ordeal* (once—2 Corinthians 8:2), *proof* (twice—2 Corinthians 9:13 and 2 Corinthians 13:3), *proven character* (twice—Romans 5:3–4), *proven worth* (once—Philippians 2:22), and *test* (once—2 Corinthians 2:9).[28]

Consequently, the Bible is describing character as not simply the possession of certain moral and admirable traits. More than that, *it is the basic structure of an individual from which those traits flow.* This means not just expressing moral qualities, but genuinely *being* a moral person. This is the essence of authentic leadership and reflects the Bible's unique proposition about leadership—namely, that we lead from who we are.

This being true, the biblical leader must consider something deeper than merely looking the part. Instead, he or she must seek to authentically take on the character of Christ in leadership. The question then is not what Jesus *did* as a leader, but who he was—in his life and in his leadership. As Jesus lived and led, so must we.

These metaphors given by the Bible help us grasp Scripture's teaching on the character of Christlike leaders. They also describe a leader's ideal view of particular, important spheres associated with leadership:

The leader as *servant* describes the leader's view of people.
The leader as *steward* describes the leader's view of power.
The leader as *shepherd* describes the leader's view of position.

The Servant: The Leader's View of People

> And there arose also a dispute among them as to which one of them was regarded to be greatest. And He said to them, "The kings of the Gentiles lord it over them; and those who have authority over them are called 'Benefactors.' But it is not this way with you, but the one who is the greatest among you must become like the youngest, and the leader like the servant. For who is greater, the one who reclines at the table or the one who serves? Is it not the one who reclines at the table? But I am among you as the one who serves. (Luke 22:24–27)

In Luke 22, the disciples are discussing a question prominent even in to-day's world: "Who is the greatest?" Humans are obsessed with greatness and the power and privilege that accompanies it. The problem for the disciples is that they did not define greatness as Jesus did.

For Jesus, greatness is measured by a different standard. To be great in God's economy is to love, empower, and serve others. In leadership, greatness means using power for others, not for self. It is found in service and sacrifice, not in perks and privileges. For biblical leaders, greatness should be measured by what God says about you, not what the world says.

Here in Luke, Jesus draws a distinction between a "Gentile" (worldly) form of leadership and that which should characterize his followers. He says that the kings of the Gentiles (i.e., leaders in positions of power and authority) "lord it over" others. Their mind-set is a top-down way of think-ing that looks upon people as below them, with the leader at the very top. Jesus said those who hold power like this are called "benefactors"—peo-ple in authority who give charitably to others but in doing so cause people to become excessively dependent upon them. Benefactors in this context are ruinous rulers who do not empower people nor help them reach their potential. Their kind of charity is more about gaining power over others and building reputation for themselves than it is about expressing true compassion or service.

Servant leaders lead for the benefit of others.
Worldly leaders lead for the benefit of self.

After describing this form of worldly leadership, Jesus said to his disciples, "But it is not this way with you!" It doesn't get much clearer! Jesus was absolutely certain that he did not want his followers to reflect the kind of attitudes and actions in leadership that figured so prominently in the world. Note the contrast in the language used:

"Gentile" View:	Jesus's View:
Kings	Greatest as youngest
Benefactors	Leader as servant
Reclines at the table	Serves at the table

In worldly leadership, leaders *ascend* into greatness through achievements that lead to "success." In servant-leadership, leaders *descend* into greatness through actions that reflect servanthood (Philippians 2:5–11). As Henry Nouwen aptly states, "The way of the Christian leader is not the way of upward mobility in which our world has invested so much, but the way of downward mobility ending on the cross."[29] In worldly leadership, perks and privileges increase as you go up in an organization. In servant leadership, responsibility and sacrifice increase as you go up. In the world's leadership, people become unduly dependent upon authoritarian leaders. In servant leadership, leaders equip, empower, and encourage others in order for them to reach their potential.

Worldly leaders might demand of others what they are unwilling to contribute themselves. Servant leaders, while certainly not required to do everything, are willing to do anything they might ask of others (John 13:1–20). Worldly leaders lead for their own benefit. Servant leaders lead for the benefit of others.

Even as God, one with all power, title, and authority, Jesus defined himself as a servant. He says here in Luke 22, "But I am among you as the one who serves" (v. 27). On another occasion, Jesus said about himself, "For even the Son of Man did not come to be served, but to serve, and to give his life as a ransom for many" (Mark 10:45). Jesus saw himself and defined himself first as a servant. It was part of his character and how he identified himself in relationship to others. Biblical leaders likewise must first see themselves as servants of others.

But many of us are uncomfortable with the notion of being a servant. We often have wrong ideas of what Jesus meant when he said that a leader should serve. We might think of servant leaders as passive and meek personalities who are required to do what others want them to do. This is a misguided view both of servant leadership itself and of the way Jesus lived it.

Just look at some of the actions of Jesus as a servant leader:

- He cleansed the temple with a whip (John 2:13–17).
- He reprimanded the Pharisees for their hypocrisy (Luke 11:37–54).
- He called people to full commitment (Luke 9:23).
- He rebuked Peter for his desire to shortcut God's plan (Matthew 16:23).
- He commanded his disciples on many occasions (John 13:34, John 15:10, Mark 12:30–31, John 18:11).

It's obvious from the list above that being a servant leader does not mean being a doormat. Instead, it means doing whatever is in the best interest of those you lead. Servant leadership is not simply defined by the action of the leader, but—and primarily—by the motivation of the leader.

Therefore, servant leaders will wash feet, show mercy, and give compassion and grace, but when necessary and in the best interest of their followers, servant leaders will also confront, challenge, and rebuke.

Servant leaders do not have to do everything.
Yet, they must be willing to do anything.

The actions of the servant leader are determined by two questions: what God would want done in the situation and what followers actually need in the situation (not necessarily what they want). The resulting actions are motivated from a heart of love, are based upon the needs of the follower, and are ultimately acts of obedience to the Father.

Servant leaders see people differently than worldly leaders do. Worldly leaders don't see people as people but as objects. They want people around in numbers but only desire to use them to achieve selfish ambitions. The servant leader, however, does not view people as objects who exist to meet the leader's needs. The servant leader comes alongside those he or she leads (and indeed comes *under* them), using his or her power, authority, and influence to meet the needs of followers and help them reach their potential. The servant leader does what is in the best interest of those he or she leads (and of the organization as a whole) and gives to them not always what they desire, nor necessarily what the leader is comfortable giving, but rather what followers *need* under the direction of Christ. Leaders do all this without abdicating their position, power, or authority.

The characteristics of servant leaders can be summed up as follows:

- They measure greatness according to God's standards, not the world's.
- They see people as people, not objects.
- They see leadership as service, not privilege.

- They are willing to do whatever is needed to serve the best interest of their followers. At times this means confronting and correcting, and at other times encouraging and comforting.
- They love those they lead. All their actions are motivated by love.
- They are not passive or weak.
- They view leadership primarily as obedience to the Father.

The Steward: The Leader's View of Power

Have this attitude in yourselves which was also in Christ Jesus, who, although He existed in the form of God, did not regard equality with God a thing to be grasped, but emptied Himself, taking the form of a bond-servant, and being made in the likeness of men. Being found in appearance as a man, He humbled Himself by becoming obedient to the point of death, even death on a cross. For this reason also, God highly exalted Him, and bestowed on Him the name which is above every name, so that at the name of Jesus every knee will bow, of those who are in heaven and on earth and under the earth, and that every tongue will confess that Jesus Christ is Lord, to the glory of God the Father. (Philippians 2:5–11)

One famous line from the movie *Braveheart* comes from a confrontation between William Wallace and the nobles of Scotland (those with land, wealth, and power, though deeply lacking in nobility of character). Wallace said, "There's a difference between us. You think the people of this country exist to provide you with position. I think your position exists to provide those people with freedom. And I go to make sure that they have it."

With position and title almost always comes power. Power is the *ability* to direct or influence the behavior of others. Authority, similar to power, is the perceived *right* to exercise power. Let me give you an example: A man of physical strength has the power (the ability) to restrain someone.

A police officer, on the other hand, has the authority (the assigned right) to restrain someone.

But there is a another component of power to consider. While one with power and authority may be *able* and *authorized* to influence another, he or she may lack the *credibility* to do so—meaning that he or she lacks moral permission from the person in question to exercise influence. From a biblical view, power without credibility is illegitimate power. Jesus possessed all power and authority. Yet, through his character and behaviors, he gained the credibility to yield power and authority legitimately. His credibility resulted from the way he used power. Ironically, by defying conventional applications of power, he gained *more*—certainly, Jesus is the most influential man who has ever lived, even down to this day.

Power, and a leader's use of it, gains or destroys the legitimacy
of his or her leadership.

Why is this discussion of a leader's power so important? Because power is possibly the greatest asset of leadership. It provides leaders with the potential to do good or bring harm. Power allows leaders to build trust and thus gain the voluntary and legitimate permission of people to influence them, or power can be used in such a way that it undermines trust and legitimacy. "Nothing is more useful than power, nothing more frightful."[30] Since this is true, the way a leader uses power is the truest test of his or her character. It unveils how a leader views himself and his assumptions about why his leadership exists in the first place.

Some begin to believe they have the right to spend the asset of power on themselves. This is because they assume their power is the result of who they are—a product of their own competence, efforts, or aptitudes—rather than a gift on loan from God. Consequently, power may be used by leaders to bless others or to promote self. Since power is inherently entrusted to leaders, and since it has the potential to bless or destroy, it is vital for biblical leaders to view it properly and manage it responsibly.

The Stewardship of Power

The Random House dictionary defines a steward as "a person charged with the responsibility of managing another person's assets that have been entrusted to his or her care." This definition reflects exactly who Jesus was in his leadership and describes his relationship to the notion of power. He understood that his work on this earth, and the power accompanying that work, were granted to him from the Father, and he viewed himself as a steward of it.

> All authority in heaven and on earth *has been given to me.* (Matthew 28:18, NIV)

> For the works which the *Father has given Me* to accomplish—the very works that I do—testify about Me, that the Father has sent Me. (John 5:36)

> The cup which the *Father has given Me,* shall I not drink it? (John 18:11)

Because of Jesus's steward mind-set, he was able to hold his power and authority as it should be held and use it for the sake of others, even though he was the very Son of God.

Pontius Pilate, by contrast, had a very different perspective about his power as a Roman governor. Jesus reminded him that no leader, no matter how great, is granted power apart from the dispensation of God:

> So Pilate said to Him, "You do not speak to me? Do You not know that I have authority to release You, and I have authority to crucify

You?" Jesus answered, "You would have no authority over Me, unless it had been given you from above." (John 19:10–11)

In Philippians 2:5–11, the apostle Paul describes the amazing truth of God becoming man in Jesus, taking the form of a servant, and being resolved to absolute obedience to the Father. Here, the whole idea of a biblical leader's use of title and authority is affirmed.

Paul says that Jesus "did not consider equality with God something to be *grasped* [i.e., "clung to," "adhered to"], but emptied himself." In other words, the very thing that Jesus could have used for his own advantage, he released. This does not mean he stopped being God. The text is describing his use of that title and authority, not the abdication of it. It did not go away, he did not lose it, and he did not apologize for it. He was God. He knew that. And he knew he had the right, power, and authority to do whatever he wanted as God. Yet amazingly, the one with all power and right to be served by others set aside that power and right in order that he might become the one serving. Never do you see Jesus use his power and authority for his own benefit! Rather, he expressed the magnanimous and moral power of power by using it for the sake of others.

Power is a stewardship on loan from God to be used
for his glory and for the good of others.

Do you know leaders who are always reminding others of their title and their power? Who cling to it obsessively? Who feel it gives them the privilege to do what they want? Jesus did not consider his title even as *God* something to be clung to or used for his own advantage. Instead, as Paul says, he "emptied himself," opting instead to use that power for the good of others.

This is why God gives power and position—for the sake of his people, not for the privilege of the leader: "And David knew that the Lord had established him king over Israel, and that he had exalted his kingdom for the sake of his people Israel" (2 Samuel 5:12).

Similarly in John 13, the night before his betrayal and arrest, Jesus displayed for the disciples what one with power and title does with it when that one is walking in God's will:

> So when He had washed their feet, and taken His garments and reclined at the table again, He said to them, "Do you know what I have done to you? You call Me Teacher and Lord; and you are right, for so I am. If I then, the Lord and the Teacher, washed your feet, you also ought to wash one another's feet. For I gave you an example that you also should do as I did to you. Truly, truly, I say to you, a slave is not greater than his master, nor is one who is sent greater than the one who sent him. If you know these things, you are blessed if you do them." (John 13:12–17)

The interplay between the titles of Jesus listed here and how he exemplifies the use of those titles is interesting: "You call me Teacher and Lord, and you are right for so I am." Jesus does not apologize for his title or authority, and he doesn't correct the disciples for seeing him that way. But he demonstrates that it is possible for authority and service, as well as power and humility, to coexist in paradox within a leader. These traits do not necessarily stand opposed to each other.

Jesus goes on to describe the way a leader uses title and power for the sake of others: "If I then, the Lord and the Teacher, washed your feet, you also ought to wash one another's feet. For I gave you an example." He then describes how a leader should view his place and position by noting that all are under authority of some sorts: "Truly, truly, I say to you, a slave is not greater than his master, nor is one who is sent greater than the one who sent him." He closes by sharing the promise of the blessing that will come to leaders who use power this way: "If you know these things, you are blessed if you do them."

We should note that while Jesus properly managed his power, there were certainly temptations for him to use it for himself. In Matthew 4, he was led by the Spirit into the wilderness to be tempted by the devil. Throughout the account, the nature of Satan's temptation in this experience is toward the abuse of power.

Satan first entices Jesus to turn a stone into bread. Jesus had fasted for forty days up to this point. His hunger was an obvious, legitimate human need. Since he was hungry, he could have rationalized that turning the stone into bread was his right, particularly as the one Son of God and as one with the power to make it happen. This scenario is the perfect storm: one in authority having a legitimate need, feeling a right to have that need met, and having the power to make it happen—incentive, rationalization, and ability. This is exactly the kind of situation where leaders make moral blunders. In an interview with Dan Rather, Bill Clinton said he had an affair with Monica Lewinsky "just because I could." But in his temptation, Jesus understood that not even a legitimate need should be met in illegitimate ways. It was not God's timing, nor was it the way that God wanted to meet this need. In this instance, turning the stone into bread would have been an abuse of his power. Jesus knew this and resisted the temptation.

The hardworking pastor who has legitimate financial needs may justify an abuse of power by taking money from the church offerings. He might say, "I work so hard for this church, and they don't pay me as they should," or "My family has needs, and look at all I have given to the church." His needs may be real, and his rationalizations may be accurate. He does have financial needs, his family should be provided for, and he might work very hard for the church. Yet, no matter how legitimate, those needs must not be met illegitimately. *With incentive, rationalization, and opportunity comes the abuse of power.* Jesus withstood that temptation.

The proper use of power means that even legitimate needs
not be met in illegitimate ways, nor before God's timing.

Next, Satan tempts Jesus by telling him to cast himself off the temple
and let the angels catch him. The devil in fact props up his perversion
with Scripture (Psalm 91:11) in order to make his point and illustrate what
leaders do—they prove their power in very public ways! The only point of
jumping off the temple was to display power and to command others in
the exercise of that power. It was to wield power for power's sake. This was
the essence of the second temptation—to put on a grand display of the
power Jesus held. Jesus resisted.

Finally, in the third temptation Satan appeals to the very real human
desire for power in the form of material acquisition—one of the common
results of an abuse of power.

> Again, the devil took Him to a very high mountain and showed
> Him all the kingdoms of the world and their glory; and he said to
> Him, "All these things I will give You, if You fall down and worship
> me." (Matthew 4:8–9)

On this side of heaven, in an opportunity consistent with Jesus's human
nature and the craving of the flesh within it, Jesus could have sought to
acquire material fortune. He could have jumped on the prospect of having
something of great material value to call his own rather than serving as a
steward throughout his entire human existence with everything only on
loan to him. But Jesus, having the attitude of a steward, knew that all the
kingdoms of the world were not ultimately the property of anyone but the
Father. He knew too that Satan, as the prince of this world, only temporarily possessed the earthly realm. He did not own it. It was merely on loan to
him from God above. Despite appearances, Satan did not have it to give
in the first place.

Notice the phrase the devil uses in the first two temptations: *"If you are the Son of God."* In other words, "You say you are the Son of God, but you're not acting like it. Do these things and you will prove yourself, validate your title, and give evidence of your authority to all." But Jesus chose not to use his power in this way. Why not? Because when you have power and authority and are secure in it, you do not have to prove it to others. Only insecure, self-minded leaders must prove their power.

Steward leaders view power differently. They don't define themselves by it. They don't spend it on themselves, and they don't believe it's theirs by right or by their own doing. Rather, power comes to them by grace and on loan from God. It is to be held as a sacred trust bestowed by the Master to be used in obedience to him as he instructs and for the sake of others. The steward leader holds power humbly, fully aware of its corrupting potential. This may be the greatest virtue of true biblical leaders: namely, that they resist the temptation to spend power on themselves.

Possession or Ownership?

The apostle Paul certainly understood stewardship and saw himself in this light. He recognized that his followers did not belong to him, that his ministry was not ultimately his, and that nothing he had accomplished was truly to his own glory (1 Corinthians 1:11–15). *In other words, he was not codependent upon the church or his lifestyle of ministry.* God had given him everything, including his ministry. God could give or take it away, and certainly God was the one to provide for and preserve it. Paul therefore could let it go.

Steward leaders do not see churches as their own, followers
as belonging to them, or ministry as something
dependent upon their power.
In truth, steward leaders can let go.

Years ago I used to think that my church was dependent upon me—my gifts, my efforts, my teaching. In reality, I was codependent upon the church. Only after facing several hardships and a real sense of failure did I get to the point of saying, "God, here is *your* church. If you want it to exist, that's up to you. It's not mine, it's yours. I trust you with it, and I will be a faithful steward of it, but I let it go." This was exactly where God needed me to be. Now, the church could flourish under God's supernatural work as I got out of the way and was freed from the burden of my "ownership."

In Corinth, people tried to elevate Paul to an improper place of ownership and ascribe to him the credit and loyalty due only to Christ. He deflected those attempts by reminding followers that he was only a steward of the ministry God had given him:

> Now I exhort you, brethren, by the name of our Lord Jesus Christ, that you all agree and that there be no divisions among you, but that you be made complete in the same mind and in the same judgment. For I have been informed concerning you, my brethren, by Chloe's people, that there are quarrels among you. Now I mean this, that each one of you is saying, "I am of Paul," and "I of Apollos," and "I of Cephas," and "I of Christ." Has Christ been divided? Paul was not crucified for you, was he? Or were you baptized in the name of Paul? I thank God that I baptized none of you except Crispus and Gaius, so that no one would say you were baptized in my name . . .
>
> For when one says, "I am of Paul," and another, "I am of Apollos," are you not mere men? What then is Apollos? And what is Paul? Servants through whom you believed, even as the Lord gave opportunity to each one. I planted, Apollos watered, but God was causing the growth. So then neither the one who plants nor the one who waters is anything, but God who causes the growth. (1 Corinthians 1:11–15, 3:4–7)

These passages reveal an additional insight about steward leaders. They view their primary function as *being faithful*. This as opposed to an obsessive focus on fruit—results, outcomes, and the like. Steward leaders commit themselves to faithfulness and by faith trust God with the fruit that results: "I planted, Apollos watered, but God was causing the growth." Worldly leaders, on the other hand, must have certain outcomes to feel good about themselves and see themselves as effective leaders. They must have a response from others. They must have growth and numbers and results.

Steward leaders concern themselves
with being faithful, not fruitful.
Faith and faithfulness are our work. Fruit is God's work.

Steward leaders define success not by fruit but by being obedient and faithful to the call of God. They then witness God bringing fruit to growth and maturity and ascribe to him the proper praise.

There may be no better illustration of stewardship and its importance to God than the parable of the talents in Matthew 25:14–30. This passage describes how three servants were given a vast amount of wealth by their master and were charged to put the assets to use. Their job was to simply invest what was given to them. Notice there are no no-talent people in the story. God has given everyone something to steward. The servant with five talents went and invested them and got a return on the investment. The one with two talents did the same, with the same result. However, the servant with one talent went and hid it. He did nothing with what the master had given him.

When the master returned, there was an accounting. To the ones who were faithful to use the assets entrusted to them, the master gave this amazing commendation: "Well done, good and faithful servant!" Notice: the commendation is not "good and *fruitful* servant." These men were commended for their faithfulness, not primarily for the increase that resulted. However, the one servant who was given the least amount and who hid the talent in the ground was judged by the master as "wicked and lazy." His condemnation was not that he did something bad with the talent, but that he did nothing with it. He was unfaithful in his stewardship.

Likewise, steward leaders have been given something precious and powerful by the Master. Our leadership positions, roles, authority, and power are valuable assets that are entrusted to our care. They are to be put to use in obedience to God for the betterment of others. Steward leaders trust God with the results of their obedience, understanding that any eternal outcomes will result only from God's power. We are merely vessels of blessing whose greatest joy comes in simply being faithful. What steward leaders seek most is that day when the Master says to them, "Well done, good and faithful servant."

The characteristics of steward leaders can be summed up as follows:

- They view leadership and the power that accompanies it as a sacred trust from God.
- They resist the temptation to spend power on themselves.
- They do not believe followers belong to them, nor do they see ministry as theirs.
- They can let go of ultimate responsibility for their churches and ministries.
- They are able to loosely hold position and title just as Jesus did and not define themselves by it.
- They focus on faith and faithfulness rather than fruit.
- They can authentically give credit to God because he is the one who causes increase.

The Shepherd: The Leader's View of Position

I am the good shepherd. The good shepherd lays down his life for the sheep. The hired hand is not the shepherd and does not own the sheep. So when he sees the wolf coming, he abandons the sheep and runs away. Then the wolf attacks the flock and scatters it. The man runs away because he is a hired hand and cares nothing for the sheep. I am the good shepherd; I know my sheep and my sheep know me—just as the Father knows me and I know the Father—and I lay down my life for the sheep. (John 10:11–15)

When Jesus defined himself as the good shepherd, he was speaking of his character. This dimension of who he was had significant meaning to the people of his day due to the prominent agricultural environment around them, and it holds important application for those of us who would lead like Christ in today's world.

There may be no more natural or obvious imagery of leadership than that of a shepherd. The shepherd is quintessentially a leader. He oversees, protects, and guides his sheep.

Shepherds direct their sheep to places of nourishment, rest, and shelter. They go before the sheep, leading the way and guiding them over terrain, through the elements, and to places ahead that are best for them. Shepherds also protect their sheep from harmful animals and elements. When danger comes, shepherds put the sheep above their own interests by standing between them and that which seeks to harm.

The shepherd initiates action, walks before the sheep, sacrifices first, and provides an example. The sheep follow the shepherd. On occasion, through difficult terrain or threatening weather, the shepherd walks with and among the sheep. He is not removed from or distant from them but provides a presence in their midst. Though not one of the sheep, he positions himself with and among those he leads.

The biblical leader views his or her position toward followers as that of a shepherd. The biblical leader's position is to walk before people, and in times of trouble or doubt to walk *with* them—not behind them or distant from them. The shepherd does not *drive* the sheep, he *guides* them. The same is true for the biblical leader. In guiding, biblical leaders go before their people; they model behavior, set the pace for advancement, and are in position to lead in the direction all should go. They direct their people to a future that lies ahead. By their care, sacrifice, identification, and hard work, they inspire others to follow. Biblical leaders don't simply point the way; they lead the expedition and by example guide people to places of blessing.

Shepherd leaders do not drive their followers;
through example, they guide them.
They don't point the way; they walk the
way and ask others to follow.

The shepherd motif denotes proximity. The leader is close to his or her followers, understanding that one might be able to impress from a distance but can only truly impact from up close. Shepherd leaders walk the places they ask others to walk, endure the same challenges on the journey, and go before others with courage and wisdom. They do not demand of others what they are unwilling to do themselves.

Additionally, just as a shepherd, biblical leaders must protect their followers from harmful people and guide them away from harmful places. The shepherd protects the flock. Pastors and elders (and indeed anyone pursuing biblical leadership in any organization) must embrace their role as protector. There are destructive, harmful people who come into churches and organizations who either willfully or unintentionally divide the body, divert from mission, and wound individuals. The protection theme speaks to the need for courage on the part of leaders to stand up to whatever opposes the sheep or seeks to lead the flock astray.

Possibly most important in John 10 is Jesus's statements about the shepherd's *heart*. Jesus describes himself as the "Good Shepherd" and more deeply qualifies that title by saying that he is the type of shepherd who:

- Sacrifices for those he leads ("lays down his life for the sheep")
- Protects them at all costs as they are vulnerable to harm caused by others ("the wolf attacks the flock and scatters it")
- Genuinely cares for those he leads ("more than a hired hand who cares nothing for the sheep")
- Builds intimacy and connection with followers ("I know my sheep and my sheep know me")

Of the three images of leadership exemplified by Jesus, one reason the shepherd image is so often applied is that the Bible itself applies it to church leadership. Peter writes to elders:

> Therefore, I exhort the elders among you, as your fellow elder and witness of the sufferings of Christ, and a partaker also of the glory that is to be revealed, shepherd the flock of God among you, exercising oversight not under compulsion, but voluntarily, according to the will of God; and not for sordid gain, but with eagerness; nor yet as lording it over those allotted to your charge, but proving to be examples to the flock. And when the Chief Shepherd appears, you will receive the unfading crown of glory. (1 Peter 5:1–4)

This text above was written by the same man who, after his three denials of Jesus, was charged by the Savior to possess a shepherd's heart for the ones he led. On the beach after the resurrection in John 21:15–17, Jesus asked Peter three times, "Peter, do you love me?" To each question, Peter replied, "Yes." Jesus then said, "Peter, if you love me . . . tend my lambs . . . shepherd my sheep . . . tend my sheep."

As the apostle penned his message to the church elders, he must have hearkened back to that eventful moment. It was a challenge from the Savior to Peter to spend his life, out of love for Christ, caring for and protecting those who mattered so much to Jesus—namely, his sheep. Peter in turn challenges church elders in his day as well as leaders in our day to "shepherd the flock of God."

One more thing to point out. Jesus told Peter in John 21 to care for *my* lambs." The people we lead belong to God, not to us as leaders. Likewise, Peter told the elders in 1 Peter 5 to "shepherd the flock of God." They are not our sheep, nor our flock. They are God's. This is yet another example of the mind-set of stewardship that accompanies all biblical leadership.

The characteristics of shepherd leaders are summed up as follows:

- They view their leadership as being like a shepherd who guides and protects their sheep.
- They position themselves in front of and among those they lead— walking with and ahead of them, not behind or distant from them.
- They guide the way, not merely point the way. They go where they expect others to go.
- They protect the ones they lead from harmful people and places.
- They genuinely care for and get to know their followers.
- They are willing to sacrifice themselves for the sake of the ones they lead.

The Character of a Leader

Leadership reveals character, builds character and tests character. This core disposition (i.e., character) lying within leaders is therefore of first importance. When leaders today choose to define themselves as servants, stewards and shepherds, and when under the sanctifying power of the Holy Spirit they are transformed in character into such, then the external traits that accompany these Jesus-like images will be more naturally expressed. Traits that are respected and desired by followers. Traits such as honesty, authenticity, courage, altruism, determination, love, security, sound decision making, perseverance, and integrity. These things, traditionally defined as "character," become the outer, organic expression of hearts that have been shaped into those of servants, stewards, and shepherds.

The result? People will trust, follow, and feel secure as the Christlike character of their leaders earns them the credibility to lead as a true biblical leader.

Chapter Review Questions

1. Do you agree that the greatest crisis in leadership today is a crisis of character? Explain.
2. Share an example of a leader who had skill but lacked character. What happened to that leader and to the organization he or she led?
3. This chapter lists many destructive results of leaders void of inner character. Name at least one that you identity and struggle with. Explain why.
4. What's the deepest meaning of character beyond the mere expression of external traits?
5. What are the three images of character as witnessed in Jesus's leadership and the sphere of influence associated with each one?
6. How does a servant leader view people?
7. Describe the difference between a "Gentile" (worldly) form of leadership and how Jesus defined true leadership.
8. Does being a servant leader mean being passive or weak? Explain.
9. What's the difference between legitimate power and illegitimate power?
10. Why is power potentially a leader's greatest asset?
11. Give an example of the abuse of power even in the context of legitimate needs.
12. What does it mean for a person to become "codependent" upon his or her churches or ministries?
13. List and explain three characteristics of a shepherd leader.

CHAPTER 4

CALLING: THE PURPOSE OF THE LEADER

*"Spiritual leadership is not an occupation, but a calling . . .
And only when Christian leaders understand leadership as a
calling by God will they be equipped to be used effectively."*
HENRY BLACKABY

If there is any single distinction to biblical leadership, setting it wholly apart from every other definition, it is the notion that there is a God in heaven who calls forth individuals to go, lead, and make a difference in this world. The idea of God's call, however, is one that has fallen by the wayside in our modern world.

This loss has occurred for two primary reasons. First, the Holy Spirit's guidance has been abused by power-hungry leaders who use it to justify their own ambitions. These leaders equate their self-centered agenda with God's will. They forbid discussion and debate about the autonomous and authoritarian decisions they make. No matter how detrimental a leader's decisions are, how does a church member challenge the statement, "God told me we should do this"?

Second, the call of God requires a unique faith complexion. A deep trust in the Almighty is necessary both for accepting the call of God and for finding the courage to act upon it, and this is disconcerting for some. Risk-averse leaders simply find it easier to go about their "jobs" without the need for hearing from God, responding in faith, and acting in courage.

Yet the Scripture is filled with example after example of people whose lives were interrupted by a call from God and who, by faith, went to lead others to achieve it. Hebrews 11:1–40 includes only a handful of them.

Those who seek to lead as the Bible describes must embrace this notion of God's call. When they do, and when they receive resolution to some of the questions associated with that call, there are tremendous benefits.

1. Real courage. Some leaders express a form of courage that is self-deceiving. False courage is not based upon a clear and accurate sense of God's call. Rather, it is a dangerous and odd mixture of a leader's selfish ambition and noble desires to expand the kingdom of God. Without ever coming to understand the inner motivations for leading others, these leaders use the commands of God as a way of meeting inner needs for power, approval, or the admiration of others. They mistake their obsessive and compulsive drive for the passion that should accompany the gospel.

Here, the legitimate objective of building the kingdom is made illegitimate by the leader's need to achieve certain outcomes. In essence, they are doing God's will, but doing it in their flesh. These individuals determine that they must have the courage to demand that others conform, to stand up to any resistance against their agenda, and to risk everything in order to achieve the outcomes they so desperately must have. False courage is presumption, not faith. It is testing God, not trusting him; getting ahead of him rather than walking with him.

> False courage is presumption, not faith. It is testing God,
> not trusting him; getting ahead of him
> rather than walking with him.

Courage is a key trait of biblical leadership, but false courage deceives a leader. It's not enough to do God's will. Biblical leaders must do God's will God's way. False courage does not flow from obedience to the call of the Father, but rather from deep insecurity. Here is an individual who must prove himself right—or more accurately, he must not be proven wrong.

Yet when leaders attain a clear and accurate sense of call from God— one that is founded upon a proper theology and a truthful view of self and that brings distinct guidance as to what God wants to do in this world— the result is real courage. Leaders then determine to remain true to their calling, and they do so with moral standing. It is real courage to remain faithful to God despite challenges and hardships and to inspire others to the same kind of faithfulness.

2. Purpose. Years ago, after the initial invasion in the Gulf War, I was watching a news program in which a former military general was interviewed. The reporter asked, "After a resounding victory in the invasion, what are some things those in military leadership need to be concerned about?"

The general answered, "What's most important as we move forward is that we must avoid mission drift." Pressed for further explanation, he defined the term: "Mission drift is when we forget the reason we're fighting in first place." It was a stunning statement and one that I immediately applied to church leadership.

In the initial stages of leadership, calling and vision are predominant, but there is a natural tendency to drift away from original motivations and purpose. Over time, needs surface that result in programmatic and even bureaucratic elements being set in place. Leaders get busy doing things that may be good but are not the things that are most effective in relation to their calling. They then forget why they are fighting in the first place.

Before leaders can find their *way*, they must first find their *why*. A clear and accurate calling of God directs the leader's efforts toward what matters most. Calling answers the question of "Why am I doing this?" with "Because God called." With the clarity of the call comes a potency to the call, a potency that protects leaders from forgetting the priorities necessary for the achievement of their mission. Biblical leaders remember that activity does not necessarily mean productivity, and effort does not necessarily mean effectiveness. Those who have a sure sense of call are able to concentrate more fully on the achievement of their mission by clearing distractions and overcoming obstacles to it.

Someone once said, "It's easier to say no when there is a deeper yes within." Biblical leaders are empowered to say no to the unimportant because of the deeper yes of God's call.

Before a leader finds his way, he must first discover his "why."
Calling answers the question of why with "Because God called."

---

3. Perseverance. Let's face it: leadership is challenging, and when leaders determine that they will practice *biblical* leadership, the Enemy gets involved. However, when one possesses a clear and accurate call from God, he or she is more equipped to endure. When times are difficult, these leaders come back to answer the most basic question of their leadership: "Why am I doing what I am doing?" If a leader is leading for any other reason than the call of God, in time those reasons will be insufficient to motivate the leader to endure.

Years ago I was part of a group called the Metro Youth Ministers Association. It was comprised of youth pastors from the fifty largest Southern Baptist churches in the nation. One year the conference was held in Houston and was led by Louie Giglio. Louie described what he termed "The Call Quotient": the difference between why a person initially went into ministry and why they were currently in ministry. He said, "Some of you are not in ministry now for the same reasons you were when God called. Your heart has changed and not for the better."

Wow! God used this to speak to me at critical time in my life. Initially, I went into ministry out of a calling to simply serve God and see people come to Christ. But over time, ministry to me became more about prestige among my peers and the size of the church in which I served. In truth, I had drifted from the call of the God and the motivations I initially had. God used that conference to return me to my original purpose and a newfound conviction to remain true to it. You see, there are some reasons for leading that allow greater endurance when overwhelming challenges occur—money and prestige fall short.

Leaders who are not driven by God's call are leaders who are apt to quit. When they do, they miss out on the experience of benefiting from the investment of all their hard work. In essence, leaders who give up pre-empt God of the opportunity to grow them in faith and character as well as to bring eventual change in the people they are leading. Jimmy Draper says, "The lack of certainty of a divine call to the ministry is one of the main reasons why approximately one-half of seminary students leave the ministry within 5 years after leaving the seminary. Without the assurance of God's call on your life you will not make it in ministry! The ministry is a terrible vocation, but it is a wonderful calling!"[31]

I have a friend who sensed a particular call of God to move from Texas to pastor a church in California. It was a church with a long history of poor leadership and dysfunction—yet he was sure of the call to go. Several months after arriving, the reality of this difficult leadership challenge set in. Some of the people (even key leaders) were resistant to his vision of making the church a more healthy, biblical congregation. He was tempted to give up. After my experience of pastoring the same church for eighteen years, my advice to him was simply this: "Outlast them!" I told him that if he would not give up on God's call, in time people would either change or leave. I stated that if God had called him there and had not called him to leave, then God would provide, and he should not give up on what God was yet to do—that the Almighty had things to teach his people and ways to grow the pastor himself.

Now, after three years, the church has seen some wonderful (though difficult) changes. Some of the people were willing to adjust, and others simply left. This pastor offered change in the right way for the right reasons and according to God's call. In time, God brought about the changes necessary through the process necessary. My friend's calling, character, and courage are finally paying off.

Ultimately, leadership means being obedient to the will of God and committing oneself to a lifetime of living for an audience of one.

---

4. Integrity. The greatest personal fulfillment inherent in God's calling is the deep sense of integrity gained as a result of staying true to it. Calling, when clear and accurate, provides an inner power leading to a conviction that says, "I will die doing what God wants." Frankly, we are missing much of this among Christian leaders today. Here, the leader's faithfulness is directed toward the Father and flows from obedience to him. The person called understands that life on this earth is brief and that the years God has given him or her must be leveraged toward what God wants. Biblical leaders do not live for the temporary pleasures afforded through positions of leadership. Rather, they have a clear sense of what is truly their "business," and by default, what is none of their business. The result of living in such a way is a feeling that they have stayed true to their most deeply held value. They live and lead for an audience of one. These are people who end their lives with few regrets regardless of the outcomes gained.

In the closing weeks of his life, the apostle Paul reflected upon his leadership. He made a great statement of personal fulfillment and integrity in 2 Timothy 4:7–8, one that every biblical leader should aspire to make themselves:

> I have fought the good fight, I have finished the course, I have kept the faith; in the future there is laid up for me the crown of righteousness, which the Lord, the righteous Judge, will award to me on that day; and not only to me, but also to all who have loved His appearing. (2 Timothy 4:7–8)

What Is a Call to Leadership?

In the Bible when God had a task to be completed or a future state he desired for his people, he called an individual to go lead others in order to bring it to pass. Yet, when we talk about a call to leadership, we're not necessarily describing a voice from heaven, a blinding flash of light, or a burning bush. Callings to leadership in the Scripture came in both subtle and overt ways. Moses had a rather dramatic calling through the burning bush. Likewise, God came to Abraham and spoke explicitly to him in an audible voice. On the other hand, Esther felt an inner prompting from God, moved by the need of the Jewish people under threat of extermination. Nehemiah learned about the broken walls of Jerusalem, and after months of prayer, he sensed the strong conviction that God wanted him to lead the effort to rebuild the walls and restore the Jewish faith.

Not only does calling come in different forms, it is also felt to different degrees. There are some things in the Christian life that don't involve "Calling" with a capital C. For example, there are clear commands in the

Scripture that we are simply to obey. All Christians are "called" in this sense. We are all called to pray, express love and kindness, give faithfully, confess sin, share the gospel, and serve others. These are matters of simple obedience, already taught clearly in the Bible, and they indicate a call to Christian duty. Other callings are unique promptings of the Holy Spirit felt during the course of walking in Christ. These may include a special leading of God to give money to a particular person or a cause, to attend a particular college, to go and speak to someone about an important matter, or to take on a task of some kind.

A call to leadership is different from general Christian obedience or momentary urgings of the Holy Spirit. A call to lead is characterized as a unique prompting of God to be used by him *to influence others* in order to achieve some kind of God-honoring future. It is specifically a prompting to lead others. It is an inner sense that God wants to distinctively use me not to simply achieve a task, but to invest in and transform the lives of people so that together we might reflect the glory of God on the earth.

This calling to influence may be fulfilled by assuming a position or title. It can also be achieved by simply being used where you are and as you are through the power of personal leadership. Biblical illustrations include people such as Abraham, Moses, Joshua, David, Esther, Nehemiah, John the Baptist, Peter, Paul, and many others. All accepted a call from God and took on responsibility to lead others in a transformative way.

A call to leadership is not just doing something for God.
It means a call to influence others to achieve some purpose
that brings great glory to God.

For example, the judges and kings of the Old Testament were charged by their position to lead God's people into a God-honoring future—a future filled with love for God, devotion to their calling as a nation, and an unwavering belief in the God of Abraham, Isaac, and Jacob. Some fulfilled this purpose (Deborah, Gideon, David); others did not. Some leaders accomplished this purpose through military leadership and the resulting reestablishment of the nation; others did so through political means and leadership actions. Their calling was connected to their position of leadership, and in that position, they led God's people into a future more aligned with God's ideal. Their sense of calling was captured in their God-given responsibility to lead God's people into his ideal future through their granted position. As such, that goal became the object of their trust in God.

Moses was called to be an instrument for God to deliver the Israelites from slavery. This calling involved not only the task of going, but also of seeking to influence Pharaoh and the Israelite people to cooperate with what God wanted to do.

Joshua was called by God to replace Moses and lead his people into the promised land. It was a calling to influence others to achieve God's will. God said to Joshua, "Be strong and courageous, *for you shall cause this people* to inherit the land that I swore to their fathers to give them" (Joshua 1:6, ESV, emphasis mine). It was a call to lead people.

Nehemiah was burdened by the destruction of the walls of Jerusalem, and he felt called to do something about it. This was not a task he could achieve on his own. Part of his calling involved an influence upon the Persian king and also upon the people who would help with the achievement of this objective. The Bible records no explicit audible voice from God, nor any supernatural vision that is associated with what Nehemiah sensed, and yet it becomes obvious from the first two chapters of Nehemiah that the cupbearer was not moved by just a fleeting emotion or burden. After much prayer and God's supernatural provision, he acted upon the purpose that burned within him. Prayer and the movement of God within Nehemiah marked the difference between simply feeling an emotional burden, a deep desire, or an altruistic motivation and sensing a prompting from God to accomplish a purpose that will impact and influence God's people—in other words, a calling.

The New Testament holds the best examples of a modern calling in the leadership of Jesus and the apostle Paul. Jesus was compelled to accomplish a clear objective for which he knew he had been born: the redemption of men and women through his atoning death and victorious resurrection. Consistent with this inner disposition, Jesus often made statements that expressed his sense of calling:

- "I came that they may have life, and have it abundantly" (John 10:10)
- "For the Son of Man has come to seek and to save that which was lost" (Luke 19:10)
- "I have come down from heaven, not to do My own will, but the will of Him who sent Me" (John 6:38)
- Then Pilate said to him, "So you are a king?" Jesus answered, "You say that I am a king. For this purpose I was born and for this purpose I have come into the world— to bear witness to the truth." (John 18:37)

Paul's call to leadership was similarly clear and compelling. He knew himself called to "be a minister of Christ Jesus to the Gentiles" (Romans 15:16). While he did in fact *see* a vision in a supernatural sense, it resulted in a different product than prophecy or supernatural instruction: it resulted in a certain leadership call.

About noon, O king, as I was on the road, I saw a light from heaven, brighter than the sun, blazing around me and my companions. We all fell to the ground, and I heard a voice saying to me in Aramaic, "Saul, Saul, why do you persecute me? It is hard for you to kick against the goads."

Then I asked, "Who are you, Lord?"

"I am Jesus, whom you are persecuting," the Lord replied. "Now get up and stand on your feet. I have appeared to you to appoint you as a servant and as a witness of what you have seen of me and what I will show you. I will rescue you from your own people and from the Gentiles. I am sending you to them to open their eyes and turn them from darkness to light, and from the power of Satan to God, so that they may receive forgiveness of sins and a place among those who are sanctified by faith in me." So then, King Agrippa, I was not disobedient to the vision from heaven. (Acts 26:14–19)

During the night Paul had a vision of a man of Macedonia standing and begging him, "Come over to Macedonia and help us." After Paul had seen the vision, we got ready at once to leave for Macedonia, concluding that God had called us to preach the gospel to them. (Acts 16:9–10)

Attendant to Paul's call was the need to influence others to join him in the work and to affect those Gentiles whom he sought to reach with the gospel. The call of God with respect to leadership goes beyond the mere achievement of a task. It involves the dynamic of affecting and influencing others toward the achievement of the task.

Characteristics of a Leadership Calling

1. Leadership calling comes from God to men.
It is God who should initiate any call to lead others. In the purest sense, we shouldn't choose leadership. It should choose us. This does not mean that leadership is not possible without calling. People lead and influence others all the time without being led by God to do so. However, if we are to achieve the highest form of effective biblical leadership with eternal results, it must be rooted in a deep sense of obedience to God and connected to his redemptive purposes.

Therefore, leadership calling is discerned when a leader engages in a process to determine whether this is God's will or their own. Otherwise, they will set off to go and do things of their own choosing and in their own power. The latter of course is a recipe for failure, or in the least, for achieving only temporary results. But when God calls, his power becomes actively at work within us and through us because the mission to which God calls us is what *he* desires to achieve. What God initiates, he accomplishes.

The biblical leader sees himself as receiving a call from the Father, acting in obedience to it, and depending upon God's power to achieve it. Contrast this to the one who has dreams and ambitions and goes to God making requests, seeking his approval, and asking for resources to make his or her desires a reality. When leaders see themselves as receiving a call from God rather than initiating it, then the fulfillment of the call depends upon God, not them.

2. Leadership calling begins with a spiritual need.

God prompts an individual to lead others because there is something he seeks to correct. There is a wrong in the world he wants to make right, a void he wants to fill, or a need he wants to address. Abraham was called to establish a nation; Moses was called to deliver the Jews from slavery; Jesus was called to redeem humankind; Paul was called to provide the gospel to the Gentiles. These represent things God sought to do in the world, and he called men and women to be used by him to make them happen.

Since this is true, the call to lead is often birthed in a tension between the way things are (the current reality) and the way things should be (God's ideal). It almost always begins in a sense of discontent—i.e., in the context of the negative. Upon the leader's conviction of what God wants to make right, he or she feels called and empowered by God to do something about it. The calling then transforms into a positive vision for what can be. Consequently, leadership calling always has a moral component: the call of God is what *can* be based upon what *ought* to be.

A leadership calling is not primarily about dreaming up
ministry programs or constructing buildings.
It is about meeting the real spiritual needs of people.

We must remember, however, that discontent does not always equal calling. There are many things wrong in the world and many reasons for discontent! One should sense a specific leading of God and discern that he or she is indeed the one called to go and influence others to address the problem. With courage and faith, those called to lead will step out to actually do something about problems that others will only decry.

3. Leadership calling is future oriented.

Since our world is in need, God desires to bring change to it and uses leaders to see it come to pass. Leadership calling, then, is about the realization of God's ideal future state for people as compared to their current position or condition. This means the essential role a leader plays in the achievement of God's calling is that of a *change agent*. He or she is called to bring influence upon the current state of affairs and the people associated with it. These called leaders must usher forth the character and competencies necessary to bring about a different future—one that reflects the will of God and his glory through the transformation of people.

4. A call to lead comes to a particular person for a particular purpose.

God can choose any means by which to accomplish his will, but generally, he chooses to use a willing human being to bring about God's ideal by faith. Leaders, therefore, are God's unique vessels for the achievement of mission.

Sometimes people are uniquely gifted or positioned in such a way that their specific character, personality, experiences, position, or setting provides the perfect context for them to be used by God to influence others. Examples include Joseph, Esther, and Nehemiah. While this is true, most leaders in the Scripture did not readily see how their unique place and experiences positioned them for God's use. Yet they launched out in faith—not because they felt qualified but because they desired to be obedient.

Many in the Bible were used by God not based upon their skills and competencies, but rather because of their simple willingness to be used. Let's face it—the disciples were not the most qualified individuals. But it was not their *ability* that was most important; it was their *availability*. To their credit, these men followed Jesus when others would not.

We see from the Bible that the God who begins a work *through* leaders is also a God who begins a work *in* them. He grows them as he employs them. *Therefore, the primary quality of those who are called to lead is their capacity for a growing faith, not their skills, competencies, or expertise.* As someone once said, "God doesn't call the equipped; he equips the called." Often this equipping comes in the form of character growth and the development of a greater trust in God. Consequently, accompanying the call of God is the need for obedience and courage on behalf of the one called.

5. The achievement of the leadership call is beyond the strength and resources of the leader.

In every instance of God's call in the Bible, God supernaturally provided for leaders beyond their own abilities. Within themselves, leaders in the Scripture did not have all that was necessary for any assignment. God supplied both the internal and external resources that they lacked.

Leaders who are called must embrace the fact that they do not possess everything needed for the achievement of call. They must trust in God to provide what is needed. Additionally, God doesn't supply in advance all the strength and resources needed. He provides in the present tense as resources are needed. Biblical leaders therefore must walk daily in trust as God provides for a future not yet realized. Leaders called by God will never see the full path. They are to walk it anyway.

Hudson Taylor, the great missionary to China, proclaimed the promise inherent in the call: "God's will done God's way will not lack God's resources!" In truth, God never leads us where his power cannot keep us. Leadership calling is not only initiated by God, it is also sustained and achieved through the supernatural power of God working in partnership with the obedient cooperation and faith response of the leader.

God doesn't provide everything a leader
needs in advance of the call.
He or she must have a present-tense faith that trusts God to provide
what is lacking each step along the way.

Discerning Calling

Discerning God's call to leadership is not always simple. The task of discernment is part motivation, part need, part context, and part understanding of God's eternal purposes. As with any decision regarding God's will, there are certain principles that apply: praying, reading the Bible, meditating, talking with godly counsel, and patiently listening to God. One must also consider inner motivations, confession of sin, and willingness to obey in full surrender to what God wants.

While these are common to understanding God's will, discerning a call to lead does have some distinct aspects.

Take for example Nehemiah. He was a Jew exiled into service under a pagan king. Yet he determined that he would remain faithful even in this almost hopeless situation. Such was the disposition of many Jews in exile who were greatly used by God (Joseph, Esther, Daniel, Ezekiel).

Nehemiah was rewarded for his faithfulness and character as he was selected to be the cupbearer for the king. Through the hardship of serving in exile, God placed Nehemiah in a unique position to be used in an amazing way.

One day, Nehemiah received word from his brother that the walls of Jerusalem were in ruins. Although this news did not equate to immediate action, this report about Jerusalem became the triggering event for his calling. Upon hearing it, Nehemiah was heartbroken.

> When I heard these words, I sat down and wept and mourned for days; and I was fasting and praying before the God of heaven. (Nehemiah 1:4)

The first thing Nehemiah did was go to God with his burden. He started a long, three-to-four-month process of pouring out his sadness before Yahweh. His prayer began by reaffirming to God (and possibly to himself) the character of the Almighty: "O Lord God of heaven, the great and awesome God, who preserves the covenant and lovingkindness for those who love Him and keep His commandments" (Nehemiah 1:5).

Nehemiah confessed his sin, the sins of his fathers, and the sins of the nation as a whole. Then he explicitly reminded God of the covenant that God had made with Israel through Moses. That promise was to gather back together those who were scattered and who had returned to God in their hearts. He ended the prayer by requesting divine intervention and provision in the already established relationship that he held with King Artaxerxes: "Make Your servant successful today and grant him compassion before this man" (Nehemiah 1:11).

God answered Nehemiah's prayer in chapter 2. While Nehemiah served before the king, Artaxerxes noticed the sad countenance of his cupbearer. This was risky in itself—no one was to be unpleasant before the king! Yet, we can read out of the account the personal nature of their relationship and the credibility Nehemiah had gained with the king. When asked by the king why he was sad, Nehemiah said, "Why should my face not be sad when the city, the place of my fathers' tombs, lies desolate and its gates have been consumed by fire?" (Nehemiah 2:3).

This act of courage by Nehemiah provided the context for God to work. Amazingly, the king asked Nehemiah what he wanted to do and what he needed in order to do it. Again with courage, the big moment now here, Nehemiah lifted a quick prayer to God under his breath and requested permission to go back to Jerusalem to rebuild its walls (Nehemiah 2:4–5). He also requested letters for safe passage and material resources for construction. All was supernaturally granted by God to Nehemiah through Artaxerxes: "And the king granted them to me because the good hand of my God was on me" (Nehemiah 2:8).

Nehemiah's experience provides insight for us in discerning a call to lead.

1. An awakening to spiritual need.

Have you been captured by a vision to meet a spiritual need in another person or people group? In the Scripture when God called a man or a woman to lead, there was a certain powerful realization, an awakening moment that occurred in the mind of that individual. It sometimes came after dramatic, triggering events such as a vision, an audible voice, or a crisis of some kind—the burning bush (Moses), the Jewish people facing extermination (Esther), the news about Jerusalem's walls destroyed (Nehemiah), an anointing by the prophet Samuel (David), a vision that changed the course of a journey (Paul), problems with false teachers and corrupt elders (Timothy). These occurrences became catalysts for these leaders to open their ears to hear the call of God. They awakened them in some stirring way to a spiritual need that existed in the world.

In today's context, the awakening moment might occur when an individual sees a people group without the gospel, a church not fulfilling its biblical mission, or a place where brokenness and injustice exist. Ultimately, however, the call goes beyond the urge to meet a material or emotional need. Rather, the leader sees the true spiritual void that exists behind the external need. The call of God is ultimately and always about the restoration and redemption of people in relationship to him.

Nehemiah saw something others didn't. He saw that the broken walls of Jerusalem were more than simply rocks and mortar out of place. Jerusalem was the epicenter of the Jewish faith. As Jerusalem went, so did the faith of the Jews. For Nehemiah the broken walls symbolized a broken faith, and rebuilding the walls was about rebuilding the Jewish faith.

A call to lead is where heaven and earth intersect. It is where God's will meets some real spiritual need in the world. In one sense it is particular and local—that is, it makes a difference in the lives of particular people. Yet in another sense the call of God is rooted in the universal and eternal. It is consistent with what God has done historically and wants to do eternally. So while the expression or method for carrying out a call may be new and unique, the content of calling is not. Rather, it is a part of God's overarching work in history to redeem that which matters to him—namely, people.

Leaders must be captured by a vision to
meet spiritual needs in others.
This is where biblical leadership begins and ends.
Everything else in leadership is secondary to this goal.

---

2. A sense of selection by God.

The ones called to lead not only *see* what others don't, they *feel* what others don't. They feel *responsibility from God* to actually do something. Why was Nehemiah the only one so heartbroken about the walls of Jerusalem? Why did he feel compelled to pray and ultimately to act? Why not his brothers or many of the other Jews who knew about Jerusalem's condition? It was because Nehemiah was the one uniquely called to lead in this God-honoring objective.

After witnessing the need, Nehemiah felt an inner prompting to pray. In other words, the news about Jerusalem did not mandate some kind of immediate action on his part other than prayer. At times leaders act first and then pray. Nehemiah, however, took three to four months to pray about the need, confess and affirm God's character and sovereignty, and ask for God to do something.

It was out of this context of prayer that God provided an opportunity for action. Nehemiah's request for permission to go, while courageous, was not an appendage to the context. It may not have even been a surprise to him. Rather, it was an organic act rooted in the process up to that point. He prayed and expected God to do something. When the time came, Nehemiah was ready. Thus began the great adventure.

Additionally, there was an obvious sense within Nehemiah that he had been selected by God to go. For him, there was no voice from heaven, no lightning flash or thunder. His call was founded upon a process of prayer and reflection. It was based upon a need in recognition of the unique position God had placed him in to address it. Ultimately, Nehemiah's call was by faith.

For the called leader there is indeed a sense of selection—*an obligation rooted in obedience to God.* Unlike onlookers, biblical leaders feel that not to go would be disobedience to the Father.

Clarifying Questions to Help Discern Calling:

- Do I sense a deep-seated burden about the need?
- Am I uniquely positioned and/or gifted to address the need?
- Do I feel that not to address the need would be disobedience to God?
- Am I compelled in my spirit with the desire to do something about it?

The call to lead, therefore, arises where a spiritual need in the world is combined with a sense of God's divine selection:

AWAKENING TO SPIRITUAL NEED
+ SENSE OF SELECTION BY GOD

= THE CALL TO LEAD

I was seventeen years old when I became a believer. As a young and passionate Christian, I quickly grew in my faith through opportunities in discipleship, service, and small roles of leadership in the youth group. My youth pastor had a huge influence upon my life. He modeled for me a life of joy and commitment in full-time ministry. At the age of nineteen, as I considered my future and the joy I was experiencing in serving and leading in student ministry, the prompting of the Holy Spirit led me to visualize a life spent in vocational ministry. This possibility was still so foreign to me! All my life up to two years from that point, I had been spiritually lost and unchurched. But that which was originally strange and scary to me in time became attractive, and then it grew into an inner burden. In reality, it was a faith prompting. God was calling.

In response, I began to pray. As I voiced the possibility to my youth pastor, he gave me some clarifying advice. He said, "Mike, if you can do anything else with your life and be content, then do that as opposed to ministry. But if you feel that this is something you *must* do to be obedient to God, then have the faith to do it."

This helped a great deal. I began to feel that I could do nothing else and be obedient to God. In this sense, a call of God is the last of options to other life choices. We don't choose it. It chooses us. It is the faith response to God's "Whom shall I send, and who will go for us?" (Isaiah 6:8a) As I looked at a world in need of Christ, it became obvious to me that God was selecting me, calling me out, choosing me to do something about it. I could no longer deny or rationalize away the fact that he was asking me to commit my life, by faith, to lead and influence others for Christ and to do so in the context of church ministry. "Then I said, "Here I am! Send me." (Isaiah 6:8b)

Thus, threaded through both the need in the world and the sense of responsibility within the leader is a divine voice saying, "Will you trust me to be used by me?" In every instance, leaders were challenged to leave the familiar and go to places unknown, places where their individual resources were not enough. These "places" were not always geographical in nature, but were always adventures of the heart. They were always contexts where the needs of the moment were greater than the resources of the leader. This is by design—those are the very places for God to work! In fact, the inadequacy of the leader is one of the major reasons for the adventure itself: to take us to a place where we become fully dependent upon him and not ourselves, a place where God is glorified on the earth.

Nehemiah's faith didn't end when he was given permission to go. It only began there. Constantly, from conception to completion, a faith walk accompanied his call to lead. After the work began, he faced challenges from within and without. Yet through it all, Nehemiah remained dependent upon God's strength and true to the values that inspired him to go in the first place.

A call to lead always accompanies a question from God:
"Will you trust me to be used by me?"

The Product of God's Call: Vision

When God calls an individual to lead, and when by faith and obedience that person accepts the call, he or she naturally begins to visualize what the achievement of that calling might look like. That ideal image of the future is also from God. The Lord helps the leader envision a desired future state for the people he or she seeks to influence. Leaders imagine the power of God's will being done in their particular leadership context. They begin to feel excitement and even joy over the possibilities of what could be if people would respond to and trust in the Lord. They see in their mind God being glorified, people being transformed, and conditions of immorality, injustice, or spiritual dysfunction being made right. This is the birth of vision.

Vision is a popular term in the leadership genre, as we have already discussed. It has been used to describe the mental image within a leader of a more ideal future. Churches and businesses alike have created vision statements that help focus their people toward what is most important.

However, when we look at the Scripture, we see that the actual word "vision" is rarely used in the sense it is today. The term in the Bible almost exclusively refers to supernatural revelations that are prophetic or instructive in nature. Unfortunately, Christian authors have forced portions of Scripture to fit into their preconceived ideas of leadership vision, even when there is no justification for doing so.

Take for example the oft-quoted verse Proverbs 29:18: "Where there is no vision, the people perish" (KJV). Many Christian leaders use this verse to support the importance of vision in the church. They would say that when a leader does not cast vision, the church is harmed and its decline is imminent, as it will quickly lose passion, motivation, and numeric growth. While that may be true, the question of the biblical interpreter becomes: is this reality supported by this verse? A glimpse at other translations consistently gives us something closer to the NIV's rendering, "Where there is no revelation, the people cast off restraint," or the ESV's more specific "Where there is no prophetic vision the people cast off restraint." The rarely quoted second half of the verse finishes the thought: ". . . but happy is he who keeps the law." The verse warns against rejecting prophetic revelations of God and promises happiness instead to those who honor God's commandments.

Vision is a clear image of God's ideal future that flows
from God's call to lead others.

If we are to be biblical leaders, the least we must do is interpret the Bible accurately! Misguided interpretations and applications are partly the reason for the lack of power and uniqueness of those in Christian leadership today.

That said, the principles and the precedents of the Scriptures *do* reveal a form of vision in the minds and hearts of leaders. This form of leadership vision (as opposed to prophetic vision) occurs upon the foundation of and after the experience of the call of God. *First comes calling, then comes vision.*

For example, the apostle Paul experienced a dramatic conversion. Upon that conversion, Paul sensed a deep call of God to leadership in the form of sharing the gospel with the Gentiles:

> But on some points I have written to you very boldly by way of reminder, because of the grace given me by God to be a minister of Christ Jesus to the Gentiles in the priestly service of the gospel of God, so that the offering of the Gentiles may be acceptable, sanctified by the Holy Spirit. In Christ Jesus, then, I have reason to be proud of my work for God. For I will not venture to speak of anything except what Christ has accomplished through me to bring the Gentiles to obedience—by word and deed, by the power of signs and wonders, by the power of the Spirit of God—so that from Jerusalem and all the way around to Illyricum I have fulfilled the ministry of the gospel of Christ; and thus I make it my ambition to preach the gospel, not where Christ has already been named, lest I build on someone else's foundation, but as it is written, "Those who have never been told of him will see, and those who have never heard will understand." (Romans 15:15–21)

As you can see, this calling was potent and clear, and it infused Paul's existence, inspiring him to start churches, preach the gospel in places hostile to it, clarify doctrine, and equip, empower, and encourage leaders in these newly established mission churches.

Flowing from his calling, Paul's mind was filled with the more preferable future for those he led. He saw in his mind an ideal state for those he loved and influenced. God conceived within him images of the fulfillment of God's will. And on many occasions, the apostle expressed these inspired ideas—what we would call vision—for the future of those to whom he ministered. These ideas comprise the core of leadership vision as understood from the Scripture. They are clear and compelling images of a more ideal future for God's people:

To the Thessalonians: "Just as you know how we were exhorting and encouraging and imploring each one of you as a father would his own children, so that you would walk in a manner worthy of the God who calls you into His own kingdom and glory" (1 Thessalonians 2:11–12). *Vision:* Paul envisions them walking in Christ and experiencing life in Christ in such a way that it reflects God's glory.

To the Corinthians: "Now I exhort you, brethren, by the name of our Lord Jesus Christ, that you all agree and that there be no divisions among you, but that you be made complete in the same mind and in the same judgment" (1 Corinthians 1:10). *Vision:* Paul envisions the beauty of love and unity taking place between those in the Corinthian church.

To the Philippians: "And this I pray, that your love may abound still more and more in real knowledge and all discernment, so that you may approve the things that are excellent, in order to be sincere and blameless until the day of Christ; having been filled with the fruit of righteousness which comes through Jesus Christ, to the glory and praise of God" (Philippians 1:9–11). *Vision:* Paul envisions godly character and righteousness within those believers in Philippi.

In Ephesians 3, we are given a passage that contains in succession descriptions of both Paul's leadership calling (to reach the Gentiles with the gospel) and his leadership vision for the Ephesian church:

Pauls' leadership calling: "To me, the very least of all saints, this grace was given, to preach to the Gentiles the unfathomable riches of Christ" (Ephesians 3:8).

Pauls' leadership vision for the Ephesian church: "For this reason I bow my knees before the Father, from whom every family in heaven and on earth derives its name, that He would grant you, according to the riches of His glory, to be strengthened with power through His Spirit in the inner man, so that Christ may dwell in your hearts through faith; and that you, being rooted and grounded in love, may be able to comprehend with all the saints what is the breadth and length and height and depth, and to know the love of Christ which surpasses knowledge, that you may be filled up to all the fullness of God" (Ephesians 3:14–19).

Moses was called to lead the Israelites out of Egypt. A vision for his people resulted and is recorded in the entire chapter of Deuteronomy 6:

Hear, O Israel! The Lord is our God, the Lord is one! You shall love the Lord your God with all your heart and with all your soul and with all your might. (Deuteronomy 6:4)

Joshua received a leadership calling to succeed Moses and lead the people of Israel to conquer their promised land. As a result, he expressed a compelling vision of that future to those he led:

Remember the word which Moses the servant of the Lord commanded you, saying, "The Lord your God gives you rest and will give you this land." Your wives, your little ones, and your cattle shall remain in the land which Moses gave you beyond the Jordan, but you shall cross before your brothers in battle array, all your valiant warriors, and shall help them, until the Lord gives your brothers rest, as He gives you, and they also possess the land which the Lord your God is giving them. Then you shall return to your own land, and possess that which Moses the servant of the Lord gave you beyond the Jordan toward the sunrise. (Joshua 1:13–15)

Nehemiah was called to rebuild the walls of Jerusalem and to lead a group of people to achieve this calling. A compelling vision of the future spiritual state of the remnant of Jews developed within Nehemiah, and he expressed it in connection with his calling to rebuild (the compelling future vision is contained in the phrase "then we will no longer be in reproach"):

Then I said to them, "You see the bad situation we are in, that Jerusalem is desolate and its gates burned by fire. Come, let us rebuild the wall of Jerusalem so that we will no longer be a reproach." (Nehemiah 2:17)

Benefits of Vision

We may think of calling as that which is internal and primarily related to the leader. Calling is where he or she starts in leadership. It is initial. Vision, on the other hand, is an image of what is final and achieved. Vision pertains to the external and is related to the communication, transformation, and inspiration of others. Vision is the compelling actualization of calling; it yields images of what a calling, when fulfilled, looks like. A leader with a calling from God who is able to translate that calling into a clear, concise and compelling vision is a leader who motivates others as well. When communicated properly by the leader, the vision associated with God's call inspires others to embrace the challenge of a great work.

Vision is the compelling actualization of calling;
it yields images of what a calling, when fulfilled, looks like.

---

1. Vision unites. Vision provides purpose, and therefore it allows people to cooperate with one another and become unified. This is different from tolerance. Tolerance is a passive dynamic and simply means that people put up with each other. Unity, on the other hand, is an active force characterized by love, intention, and a common vision. God wants his church not simply to tolerate each other, but to become "of the same mind, maintaining the same love, united in spirit, intent on one purpose" (Philippians 2:2).

Since the achievement of vision is larger and more important than any one person's agenda, everyone submits to and rallies around its achievement. The church community realizes that God's will is at stake, that spiritual needs must be met, and that petty differences must be set aside. Unity flows from purpose (Acts 2:42–47). In fact, without clear purpose churches cannot become unified. Calling, and the vision that flows from it, produces a clear sense of purpose that naturally brings people together in love, harmony, and motivation.

2. Vision reduces conflict. There is a direct, inverse correlation between the degree of the prominence of vision in a church and the degree of conflict in the church. Initially, while vision may actually produce conflict with those who disagree with it, in time vision has the ability to clarify purpose in such a way that unity must result.

When vision is prominent, conflict is reduced. When vision is not prominent, conflict increases. This is because when there is a void of vision, other less important priorities will take its place. If God's call does not get people's attention, something else will. It is those insignificant matters that often create conflict and disagreement. People begin to look critically at minor things in the church and at each other—at the petty and at personalities. They argue about the color of the carpet and about what the pastor said that they didn't like. As Lovett Weems states, "Without a compelling vision there will be a vacuum in which almost nothing is happening, but in which almost every problem becomes exaggerated."[32] In truth, people who do not turn their attention to the compelling nature of God's vision turn on each other.

3. Vision provides accountability. Churches are notorious for being busy, active places with plenty of programs and ministries. Yet with all the busyness, we often look around and wonder why we aren't being more effective in bringing change. Could part of the problem be that we are busy doing things that don't translate into transformation? Peter Drucker's statement applies well here: "There is surely nothing quite so useless as doing with great efficiency what should not be done at all."[33]

Once a vision is set before people, it inherently provides a means for accountability and evaluation. If vision is prominent, the accompanying question will always be, "Are we achieving it?" This is one reason why it's easier not to have any vision at all—there's no accountability when we don't. But when vision is clear and well-communicated, it becomes a measure for work, prayer, effort, and obedience to God. This helps a church not just be busy, but hold itself accountable to actually achieve God's will.

4. Vision inspires and motivates. Without a clear sense of vision, people become frustrated, burned out, and dogged by a lack of meaning in their work. They lack purpose and have no greater reason for the effort they are giving. Biblical leaders are able to contextualize the seemingly mundane things that people do in the church into the larger sense of God's vision. In the leader's mind, every person matters in the achievement of vision, and therefore what they do is important. When people understand that they are an integral part of the great unfolding of God's call, it compels them from within. Vision provides them a purpose greater than themselves and thus an inner fuel by which to serve, pray, give, love, stay up late, and get up early.

There is a story of Michelangelo during the restoration of the Sistine Chapel and his painting of its ceiling. He passed by a construction worker on the way inside and said to him, "What are you doing?" The man said,

"I am laying a brick." He walked down further and said to another worker, "What are you doing?" The worker said, "I'm building a cathedral."

There's an amazing difference between the mind and heart of a person laying a brick and that of one building a cathedral. One has vision, the other doesn't. One understands the larger purpose, the other doesn't. Biblical leaders must have the ability to help people see how their activity adds to a vision for the greater work of God. In doing this they provide hope, inspiration, and endurance to those who labor in the Lord.

As Antoine de Saint-Exupéry said, "If you want to build a ship, don't drum up the men to gather wood, divide the work and give orders. Instead, teach them to yearn for the vast and endless sea."[34]

When Vision Fails

I am often asked about those times when vision has apparently failed. People set out with a calling and vision yet do not see it come to pass. My response is this: If the vision is indeed from God, it has not failed us; rather, we have failed the vision.

Some visions fail because they were not rooted in God in the first place. Rather, they were distorted visions flowing from a leader's own dreams or desires. They may have been noble, but were essentially his or her plans, not God's vision.

God-given visions fail for various reasons, but almost all are related to the leader or leaders responsible to steward them. The success of the vision is not simply in receiving it. We learn from Abraham, Moses, Nehemiah, Paul, and others that visions must be implemented, managed, and ultimately completed in ways that honor God. God wants to use the leader not only to receive the vision but to be the primary tool used to bring it about in the world. Thus, competencies within the leader to actualize vision are vital too.

We may fail vision in many ways.

God's Will, My Way

Leaders have a way of getting ahead of God in the implementation of vision. In essence they say, "Now I have the vision, *I* will go and make it happen." Remember, visions are not only given by God, they are resourced by him. That means executing the vision at God's pace—not getting behind God due to fear and a lack of courage, but also not getting ahead of God due to presumption and impatience. God's will must be done God's way.

Poor Planning

Visions fail because leaders make poor decisions in their implementation. When applied, visions take good management, strategic thinking, and clear communication. Nehemiah is a great example of a visionary who planned well. His organized methods and wise planning undergirded the success of his vision. Leaders should likewise do the hard work of planning.

Lack of Faith

God uses vision as a way to grow a leader's faith and the faith of the people who receive it. This may be one of the most important objectives of God when he calls and gives vision in the first place: to make us dependent upon him that we may find him utterly dependable. If we lack faith and courage, we lack the essential internal resources for vision to be seen through the very end. Vision is about God's work, and leaders must see it in their minds, feel it in their hearts, and trust in God every step along the way.

Releasing the Vision Prematurely

While visions address an urgent need, they are not hasty reactions. Therefore, they should not be communicated prematurely. Nehemiah took months to pray and consider his calling and vision. Additionally, he waited patiently for the right time to unveil the vision to those who would help him implement it:

> I did not tell anyone what my God was putting into my mind to do for Jerusalem. (Nehemiah 2:11)

> Then I entered the Valley Gate again and returned. The officials did not know where I had gone or what I had done; nor had I as yet told the Jews, the priests, the nobles, the officials or the rest who did the work. (Nehemiah 2:15–16)

The Apostle Paul likewise spent three years in preparation for his ministry before launching out as a missionary and communicating vision (Galatians 1:17).

There is a pacing and a timing to vision. I've known leaders who have gone to a church conference one night, received a "vision" from God, and shared it the next morning at church with the congregation. A vision that is released prematurely like this is a vision not bathed in prayer; it is a vision where a leader has not counted the cost; and it is a vision where others have not had time to consider both its need and validity.

Poor Communication

Visions must be communicated clearly, consistently, and creatively. If visions are fuzzy, dull, unclear, or nonsensical; if they are not ubiquitous in that they don't drive decisions and practices, or become consistent topics of conversation; if they are only shared by one person in a one-dimensional way; if they only belong to the leader and not others; they will fail.

The communication of vision is vitally important in this day and age. Yet, this goes beyond mere spoken words. In a real sense, vision is caught, not taught. This means that vision must not only be *shared* through verbal words and print, but also *shown* through stories, experiences, illustrations, videos, testimonies, etc.

Making It About Self

Leaders have a way of becoming the objects of change rather than the agents of change. When leaders draw attention to themselves and make vision about their image, their ministry, and their future, then vision fails—or worse yet, it succeeds at the wrong thing. Visions, in the end, are about God and his glory on the earth.

Leaders must point people to the vision and not to themselves. They should point people to the true author of the vision, our Great God in heaven. They should remain humble enough to deflect from themselves any glory due to God. A vision like this is a vision that will last.

Lack of Integrity

Leaders cannot demand of others what they are unwilling to give themselves. Sometimes leaders communicate vision in terms of cost and sacrifice yet are unwilling to pay the price. Every vision demands a set of beliefs and behaviors on the part of the leader. He or she must be willing to give not just what others are willing to give, but more. Without such commitment, a leader lacks integrity. Without integrity, there is no trust. Without trust, people will not follow.

Giving Up

Quite simply, many visions fail because leaders quit on them. Maintaining vision becomes difficult and challenging. It demands faith and sacrifice. These hardships wear on the leader to the point where it becomes easier to simply give up. Yet leaders who give up on the implementation of vision may not have owned the vision deeply enough from the outset. Leaders must personally own the vision to the degree that they could never give up on it. In their minds it must happen and will happen with courage and perseverance.

Sometimes adjustments must be made. Maybe we've gone about vision the wrong way. Maybe we've allowed our drive for the achievement of vision to undermine our marriage and family. Maybe we've made mistakes. These things happen in ministry and during the course of living out vision. Yet almost any mistake can be redeemed and rectified by a humble and repentant leader. Vision, even in the face of failure, can be redeemed without giving it up.

Making major course corrections is not the same as quitting on vision. Our encouragement is that God uses all things—mistakes and successes alike—to form us into the image of Jesus and to teach us how to live out and live within the calling and vision he has provided. The hardships we face as we attempt to carry out vision are not necessarily random. They may in fact be necessary tools in shaping us to be the kind of leader God needs to bring this vision to others and to see it through to the very end.

Chapter Review Questions

1. Explain the concept of false courage.
2. How does a clear and accurate calling of God empower leaders to endure through hardship?
3. How is a call to leadership different from Christian obedience or momentary urgings of the Holy Spirit?
4. List three common characteristics of a leadership calling. Briefly explain each.
5. Why is it important to understand that leadership calling comes from God to men—not the other way around?
6. Explain the spiritual need that triggered Nehemiah's call to leadership.
7. Describe how one discerns God's call to lead.
8. What are four clarifying questions to help discern calling that are based upon spiritual need?
9. Explain the relationship of calling to vision.
10. What are four benefits to leader vision?
11. Explain your calling to lead. In what way has God called you to influence others for his glory?
12. List and explain three reasons why visions fail.

CHAPTER 5

COMPETENCE: THE PRACTICES OF THE LEADER

"So he shepherded them according to the integrity of his heart, And guided them with his skillful hands."
PSALM 78:72

As important as they are, Christlike character and a calling from God alone will not result in the practice of effective biblical leadership. Leaders with character and calling might be loved, but they will not be followed in the long term if they are incompetent.

For all the depth of character that he possessed, along with the calling that propelled his life, Jesus was also a skilled and competent leader. Among other things, he communicated well, understood the dynamics of culture, led change, dealt effectively with conflict, and developed those he led.

Jesus's character and calling connected to his competencies in at least two ways. First, they grounded his skills in a proper moral motivation. Because of the integrated life Jesus led, he never used his skills as a way of deceiving or manipulating others. Rather, *who he was* as a leader (his godly character and calling) was authentically connected to *what he did* as a leader (his competencies). Second, his character and calling ensured the direction of those competencies toward the fulfillment of his mission. Jesus's leadership skills were not practiced randomly or without intention. His competencies were integrated devices that led toward the fulfillment of his God-honoring purpose. His leadership skills were a means to an end. They were key instruments that expressed his character and achieved his calling.

Skills and competencies themselves have a way of attracting people to a leader. Skills impress—but when they are combined with character and calling, leaders don't merely impress others, they impact them in lasting ways. It's the difference between just being admired, as many leaders are, and being an agent of change, as leaders need to be.

Students of leadership must come to understand both the essential skills common to all effective, Christlike leadership and the skills unique to who they are as individuals. The former means that one discovers from God's Word common competencies of effective, biblical leaders. The latter means that one discovers his or her spiritual gifts, natural competencies, unique personality, and God-given passions.

This text will address five common and effective skills of leadership as found in the Scripture. Students are encouraged to seek resources outside this book that will lead them to understand their unique spiritual gifts, passions, and personalities.

When skills are combined with character and calling,
leaders don't merely impress others, they
impact them in lasting ways.

Skills Essential to Biblical Leadership

Character must be developed over time and through experiences that challenge and bring testing. Skills, on the other hand, may be learned through a willing spirit and diligence. Character is an internal growth process. Skills of the type we will examine here are assimilated from the outside in and therefore can be studied, acquired, and ultimately practiced. Leaders who are committed and teachable are leaders who can become competent in ways they naturally are not.

As we look across the New Testament, and in particular at the life of Jesus, we discover five essential competencies common to effective leadership. They stand at the forefront of leadership itself and must therefore be assimilated into a leader's practice. Said another way, unless leaders are practicing these five essentials, they may not be leading at all.

Competency #1: Effective Communication

The greatest plans and purposes of ministry cannot be achieved if they are not communicated clearly and compellingly. What a leader says and how he or she says it are powerful tools to bring life, inspiration, unity, and direction. Yet, many leaders never consciously consider how they communicate. They speak purposelessly and sometimes in ways that undermine the very things they seek to achieve.

Interpersonal Communication

Leaders constantly interact with other individuals in the course of day-to-day work. These moments, beyond allowing the exchange of information, are also wonderful opportunities to build rapport and credibility. The cumulative effect of such interactions generates within the follower a perspective about the leader. Leaders build trust and produce a sense of team and unity through these exchanges, and communication is the primary vehicle through which that occurs. Leaders who see these interactions as simply the sharing of information miss the true nature of what they mean and the potential they hold.

The book of Ephesians was written for the purpose of building unity and maturity among the members of the church in Ephesus. Paul's clear admonition in chapter 4 revolves around the qualities of unity and maturity (vv. 1–6) and enforces the key role of leaders in producing them (vv. 11–13):

> Therefore I, the prisoner of the Lord, implore you to walk in a manner worthy of the calling with which you have been called, with all humility and gentleness, with patience, showing tolerance for one another in love, being diligent to preserve the unity of the Spirit in the bond of peace. There is one body and one Spirit, just as also you were called in one hope of your calling; one Lord, one faith, one baptism, one God and Father of all who is over all and through all and in all . . . And He gave some as apostles, and some as prophets, and some as evangelists, and some as pastors and teachers, for the equipping of the saints for the work of service, to the building up of the body of Christ; until we all attain to the unity of the faith, and of the knowledge of the Son of God, to a mature man, to the measure of the stature which belongs to the fullness of Christ. (Ephesians 4:1–6, 11–13)

Throughout the rest of the chapter, Paul instructs the church in how to achieve unity and maturity—and the overriding context is the subject of interpersonal communication. These principles are important for the church as a whole, and given the context, have particular application for its leaders.

1. Communication should be compassionate.

> But speaking the truth in love, we are to grow up in all aspects into Him who is the head, even Christ. (Ephesians 4:15)

This passage is an admonition for the body of Christ to speak truth to one another. We need a commitment to truth and authenticity, and certainly this is true for leaders as well. Leaders must have courage to say what others are unwilling to say. But sometimes leaders communicate harshly and abrasively. Paul says that maturity in Christ means that when speaking the truth, we do so with the goal of love. This is opposed to the goal of being punitive or proving ourselves right. The apostle decrees the loving manner in which truth is to be spoken. He says that in communication, one can be absolutely right and even truthful and yet disobey and dishonor Christ by the attitude in which one speaks. Truth, Paul says in this passage, should be communicated redemptively—that is, with the goal of gaining the other person.

Many leaders feel they are right and truthful in what they say, yet they burn bridges in their relationships by the way in which they say it. In Christ, we don't have the right to say what we want to say however we want to say it. The Bible is clear that we must control our tongues, even when they convey truth, for they may cause great harm to others (James 3:1–12). This is particularly true of a *leader's* words. People listen more carefully to leaders and care more deeply about what they say because in the mind of a follower, right or wrong, the judgment of a leader matters more than that of other people. There is a way to speak boldly, with clear instruction and correction, yet not arrogantly or cruelly. Paul did it all the time in his ministry, and he commands it here. Our words are a sacred stewardship, and we as leaders should manage them carefully.

In communication, one can be absolutely right and even truthful
and yet disobey and dishonor Christ by
the attitude in which one speaks.

---

2. Communication should be candid.

> Therefore, laying aside falsehood, speak truth each one of you with his neighbor, for we are members of one another. (Ephesians 4: 25)

Verse 25 gives us the other side of the truth-telling coin. Whereas verse 15 is about the affirmative and active communication of truth, verse 25 concerns deceit and the passive cover-up of truth. In verse 15 Paul emphasizes voicing truth. In verse 25, with the phrase "lay aside falsehood," the emphasis is on not being deceitful. There is a subtle but important difference between actively speaking truth to others and passively withholding truth from others. Laying aside falsehood means not hiding or misrepresenting what is true and accurate.

Leaders who both speak the truth in love and do not cover up what is true are leaders who are trusted and believed. Often, leaders are great about communicating positive news but tend to whitewash negatives. They may deflect responsibility from themselves and minimize the impact of a poor decision, or they may hide disappointing news entirely, fearing that it might be perceived as a reflection of their leadership. Biblical, authentic leaders must have the kind of integrity that communicates all circumstances, good and bad, accurately and honestly. Leaders who admit it when they are wrong or could have done better can be—and will be—trusted. Leaders who tell the truth about disappointment and setbacks will be believed when good things come.

Speaking truth to others assumes a particular disposition within the leader: he or she must have a courageous commitment to objectivity by way of God's perspective. This means that leaders stand apart from circumstances, ministry, and people to see as God sees, never completely defining themselves by the positive or negative context that surrounds them.

For leaders, laying aside falsehood means that when hardship comes, they know that things are never as bad as others might think because God is always at work. Leaders stand above those moments, knowing there is always an opportunity for Christ to be glorified and always an occasion for good to come even in the most challenging times. Leaders understand that biblical solutions are the way out of any difficult situation, and that propels them to communicate truthful hope to others. In this sense, leaders are eternally optimistic. They communicate positively to their people even while acknowledging what is negative. They have an authentic way of communicating needs, problems, and responses to hardships without causing people to lose heart.

At the same time, things are never as good as some might presume. God always has a future for us to pursue on this side of heaven. There is always room for growth and improvement. There is always a vision to pursue. So while celebrating victories and successes, leaders see them as gifts of grace from the hands of God, and they recognize that successes are only temporary resting places—not final victories.

This is what it means for leaders to be driven by truth, not by circumstances or feelings. The leader consequently communicates a nonanxious presence before people when times are toughest, yet he or she never becomes presumptuous when things are good, taking false comfort in the way things are or assuming troubles will never come again.

Leaders understand that biblical solutions are the way
out of any difficult situation, and that propels them
to communicate truthful hope to others.

---

3. Communication should be current.

Be angry, and yet do not sin; do not let the sun go down on your anger, and do not give the devil an opportunity. (Ephesians 4:26–27)

The immediate application of vv. 26–27 is that when others offend us to the point of anger, we must resolve the conflict quickly. Doing so dispels anger, allows forgiveness to be exchanged, and preempts Satan's attempts to embed bitterness in our hearts. Paul's idea is for God's people to keep their anger only temporarily, because anger has a way of accumulating over time. Offenses stored up from one day to the next have a way of growing and creating resentment. What begins as something small becomes bigger when not dealt with or communicated—the proverbial molehill becomes a mountain.

But when Paul said "do not let the sun go down on your anger" in the context of building unity through speech, he also provided a great principle for communication in leadership. Leaders tend to generate anger within followers when they don't communicate in present-tense ways. As time passes, people who do not know what's going on withhold the benefit of the doubt from their leaders and may eventually become distrustful and resentful of them. Leaders who possess character and otherwise good leadership skills *but do not communicate to others on a timely basis* are exposed to needless critique. They do not "close the loop" or follow up well with people. They do not give adequate information to people at the time they need it. In the end, these leaders create a form of discontent within followers. Consequently, the devil is able to gain a foothold and undermine their leadership before others. If timely, present-tense communication occurs instead, this form of anger can be avoided.

Leaders by definition are the ones in the know, and because of this they often underestimate the need to communicate to others. Communicating in advance and replying in a timely way builds credibility, communicates value to subordinates, and gives people an empowered sense that they know enough to do their jobs. It also helps everyone feel integral to the direction of the organization.

Bottom line: leaders should communicate early and often to those affected by their decisions and actions. This means sharing the right information with the right people at the right time. Otherwise, people will start to make things up and fill in the void left by the leader. (For the flip side of this principle, see "Other Principles of Communication" below.)

4. Communication should be constructive.

> Let no unwholesome word proceed from your mouth, but only such a word as is good for edification according to the need of the moment, so that it will give grace to those who hear. (Ephesians 4:29)

A leader's words must always be edifying. While it is important to communicate *information*, there is also a need to communicate *inspiration*. Communicating constructively means speaking to the heart as well as to the mind. Good leaders learn to speak to the best of others, not to their worst. By what they say, they tap into people's sense of esteem and speak to their potential.

Leaders can underestimate the importance of this kind of communication. They feel inspired and passionate, and they presume that others do too. However, most people do not have the same level of commitment and passion a leader does, and at times, those we lead will lose heart. Leaders are driven by vision. This sustains them in powerful ways. Those we lead are driven not only by vision *but also by the leader's valuation of them.* Most people don't just follow a vision: they follow the leader embodying that vision. As the leader perceives them, so they perceive themselves. As the leader believes in them, so they believe in themselves. Speaking to the ones we lead in edifying ways is essential to effective influence. Simply put, we need to build others up by our words.

Most people don't just follow a vision:
they follow the leader embodying that vision.

Giving thanks to those we lead, speaking to them about their potential, praising them for their efforts and results, rewarding them, challenging them to reach higher, giving them the credit rather than taking it for ourselves, writing notes, giving affirmation publically—these are all valid means of edification, provided they are sincere. And of course, there are many other ways to build up others as well.

Thomas Carlyle said, "Call a man brave and you help him become so." Our words, particularly as leaders, have a profound impact upon the motivation and satisfaction of those we lead. In time, they become self-fulfilling prophecies in both our people and our organizations.

Part of edifying others means that we celebrate wins and tell success stories. Small and frequent communication of this type builds a belief system that something God-sized is going on. It ultimately forms a culture that is positive and edifying. People want to work in an uplifting environment, and they love to hear positive, real-life stories—stories of life change and God's miraculous work. Stories that illustrate the difference they are making through their service and sacrifice. These things are likely happening every week in your organization. You as the leader must *see* them—you must have a perspective of the positive work that God is doing—and then you must be conscious and committed to sharing these inspiring stories with those who follow your lead.

This skill, as all the others, points to something needed in the heart of the leader and demonstrates again the necessity of grounding what we practice in who we are. For edifying communication to be authentic, leaders must truly believe in the potential of others and see the best in them. We as leaders limit others by what *we believe* they will do and become. In essence, we supply the "no" for them in advance of the question and the opportunity. Leaders who communicate in positive and edifying ways are leaders who actually perceive people in positive and edifying ways and thus influence them to do and become more. Do you?

Organizational Communication

Not only do leaders communicate on an interpersonal basis, they must also communicate in effective ways to the organization as a whole. Here communication becomes about instructing and inspiring the entire body, not just an individual or work group. Jesus spoke interpersonally to individuals, but he also communicated to larger groups and crowds. He had a corporate vision and a set of shared ideals for the universal church, and he communicated them powerfully (see Matthew 16:18, Matthew 18:15–19, Matthew 28:18–20, John 13:35, John 17:1–26). In the establishment of the New Testament church, broad decision-making structures and communication channels were put in place. The entire church was commanded to embrace powerful messages of collective purpose, operational values, and spiritual truths.

These aspects of communication go beyond our individual interactions and into competencies necessary for corporate leadership. When the following skills and mind-sets are learned and applied, leaders have the potential to move entire bodies of people into a compelling shared future.

1. A Corporate Mind-set

"Corporate leadership" has a negative connotation in the church because we've equated the word *corporate* with *corporation*. In truth, biblical leaders must think corporately—not in a business sense, but in the sense of thinking about the whole body (*corpos* being Latin for *body*). Sometimes leaders see only the individual trees and not the whole forest. This leads them to a form of micro-leadership that keeps them overly busy and unable to see the larger picture. Biblical leaders must have the mind-set to step back from the details of the day-to-day and see where the ministry is headed as a whole. Is everyone going the same direction? What communication is necessary to move and inspire the group as a whole? Do we have a sense of shared destiny? Where does God want the group as a whole to go? What is the church's identity as a body? These are the communication questions leaders must answer if they are going to direct an entire congregation or organization in an inspired and unified way.

Biblical leaders must have the mind-set to step back
from the details of the day-to-day and see
where the ministry is headed as a whole.

---

2. The Leader as Teacher

Think back to a great teacher you had in your life. It is likely this person did more than pass information about a particular subject on to you. He or she influenced you in some powerful way, challenging you to believe something valuable about yourself and achieve something worthwhile with your life. It's true—great teachers lead. But great leaders also teach!

Anyone who holds influence over a body of people must possess the communicative skill of teaching others. People in our churches and organizations need encouragement, inspiration, equipping, comfort, vision, hope, and sometimes reprimand. The leader as teacher simply means that a leader must have the ability to identify the needs of his or her people and then communicate effectively to address those needs in spoken and/or written form. Being a great leader-teacher means:

- Organizing: Planning your thoughts, keeping your communication focused on the need(s) of your hearers, and then structuring your presentation in a logical, sense-making way. This is true for a speech, a sermon, or any written communiqué.
- Storytelling: Great stories illustrate and inspire. This portion of communication is often overlooked, and leader-teachers don't spend nearly enough time developing this important tool. Storytelling separates a good teacher from a great one and allows the one teaching not only to inform hearers, but to influence them in powerful ways. Just look at the many parables that Jesus told.
- Excellence in delivery: Great leader-teachers deliver their material with distinction and quality. Some leaders are natural at this. They speak well publically and present material in such a way that people "get it." Others must be trained and committed to improving. Either way, leaders who are unsure of their message, disorganized in thought, and/or missing a good flow and structure in their communications will lack potency in the messages they seek to send to followers.

Jesus taught in organized and sense-making ways, used powerful and insightful stories to illustrate truth, and delivered his teachings with distinction and quality. These communication skills allowed him to powerfully influence others, not merely pass data on to them. Upon completion of Jesus's first public teaching moment, the Sermon on the Mount, Matthew described his Lord as leader-teacher in this way: "When Jesus had finished these words, the crowds were amazed at His teaching; for He was teaching them as one having authority, and not as their scribes" (Matthew 7:28–29).

3. Effective Communication Processes

Leaders create structures that either help or hinder communication in the organization as a whole. It is important to minimize bureaucracies and create communication channels that allow for the free flow of information. When communication doesn't take place, ministry is hurt. This is the lesson from Acts 6:1–7. When the Hellenistic widows were being overlooked, it was simply because of a lack of communication and proper structure. The apostles changed the structure, allowing for the communication of needs to the proper people to take place. As a result, "the word of God continued to increase, and the number of the disciples multiplied greatly in Jerusalem" (Acts 6:7).

In the matter of communication processes, keep in mind that there is such a thing as information overload. Most leaders and managers are fond of saying "You can't communicate too much," but in fact you can communicate too much in two ways. First, you can communicate too much insignificant information. There is only so much information people can handle. This is the *bandwidth principle,* which says there is limited room in the minds and attention spans of people who are already overwhelmed with information. Second, it is possible to communicate too much significant, substantial information. After all, if everything is important, then nothing is. Leaders must manage the amount of information they communicate, the rate of its distribution, and who it goes to in the organization, all in light of its degree of importance. Not all information is important enough to communicate on a macro level to the entire organization. Likewise, not all information, even important information, should be communicated all at once.

Other Principles of Communication

Communication reflects who you are. Jesus said, "Out of the mouth the heart speaks" (Luke 6:45). This means the kinds of stories you tell, the attitude with which you share information, and the content of what you share or withhold—all of these things express to others not only the substance of what you're communicating, but also the kind of person you are and the beliefs you possess.

What kind of person are you? Are you negative, insistent, people-pleasing, indecisive . . . or are you empowering, visionary, optimistic, hopeful? Listen to yourself to find out, or better yet, give permission to someone to give you honest feedback by asking, "How am I seen by people when I communicate?"

The kinds of stories you tell, your attitude, and the content of what you share express to others the kind of person you are and the beliefs you possess.

Communication is complex and paradoxical. What to say and how to say it cannot always be determined in advance, nor is the question of communication one-dimensional. At times Jesus was unassuming in his communication, and at other times he was startlingly bold. He was at times comforting in his words and at other times rebuking. In some instances, he was both. For example, in John 14 he began by providing great words of hope and comfort ("Do not let your hearts be troubled, believe in God, believe also in me"), and yet just a few moments later he was confronting and forceful:

> Philip said to Him, "Lord, show us the Father, and it is enough for us." Jesus said to him, "Have I been so long with you, and yet you have not come to know Me, Philip? He who has seen Me has seen the Father; how can you say, 'Show us the Father'?" (John 14:8–9)

The lesson here is that leaders must learn the art (not simply the science) of what to say, how to say it, and when to say it. *The determination of these things is based upon the situation and the needs of the moment.* Good leaders have a sensitivity in what they say. They do not "violate the moment" but rather speak *to* it and *in* it in a way that achieves what is effective.

The issue is rarely the issue. What a person says to you and what is in reality going on in his or her heart are often two very different things. *People are more what they hide than what they show.* Leaders who only hear what people say, without listening for deeper meaning as well, are leaders who address symptoms instead of real problems.

When the rich young ruler came to ask Jesus what was necessary for him to inherit eternal life, Jesus understood in a deep way what his real question was and what his real needs were (Luke 19:16–22). This was more than a result of Jesus's foreknowledge as deity; it also came from his keen understanding of human beings in general. People often ask self-serving questions and say superficial things that have nothing to do with the attitudes or needs of their hearts. In fact, they are often not aware of their own inner needs. At other times however, people intentionally deflect attention away from needs they know they have because it's too vulnerable to be honest with someone about them. Good leaders tend to develop a sixth sense about these kinds of things, understanding that what people communicate is often subconsciously being used to promote something about themselves, gain something from the leader, or meet a deeper need that has little to do with their words.

A common scenario is that of offense: a follower may become offended and belligerent over an action or word, yet if the issue can be talked out, it will become clear that the experience has triggered something deeper that has little to do with the actual situation. Once you understand the deeper issue—the real problem—you can begin to speak to it. The results may be transformative. What occurs on the outside may be completely disconnected from the real matter at hand. The issue is rarely the issue. If we learn anything from Jesus it is this: leaders speak to the heart of the issue.

The issue is rarely the issue. If we learn
anything from Jesus it is this:
leaders speak to the heart of the issue.

Share the right information at the right time and with the right people. Leaders should develop a good "need to know" strategy for communication. We get into trouble by sharing important information with people unrelated to it. This creates a lack of confidence in the leader, especially when people associated with a decision don't have the information but others do. Leaders in this sense can become gossips. Also, when a leader shares information too early without context, people set expectations that might not be met.

Jesus had a sense of what to share, with whom to share it, and when to share it. Even with his disciples, he communicated much more information to the inner circle (Peter, James, and John) than he did to the others. This was his attempt to give information to those who most needed to know and who would do with that information what he desired. Not all information was for everyone.

The lesson here is that leaders should speak from the inside-out of an organization: start with the inner circle of leaders and then communicate outward all the way to the congregation or the people to whom you minister. What the inner circle needs to know may not be what the congregation needs to know. What the congregation needs to know, the inner circle should certainly already know. In other words, *you should never announce to the group as a whole what you haven't already shared with those closest to you.* This rule empowers those closest to you and also improves the message being sent to the outer circle as it's altered by the feedback and/or validation received from other leaders. Additionally, the inner circle become ambassadors of the message on the leader's behalf, thus increasing the potency of the message and ensuring it gets heard by as many people as possible.

Deliver on what you say or do not make commitments. When leaders don't follow through or "close the loop," they lose integrity with those they lead. If you say to your son, "I'll be at your baseball game" and then you never show up, he's not going to trust you when you speak—whether about the game or any other subject. Followers have an inherent expectation that leaders will follow through with what they say, and when they don't, they begin not to trust them. Leaders are usually sincere in the things they say. In other words, they have good intentions. *But sincerity is not the same as integrity.* A leader must follow through. It is best to remain silent if you can't. Jesus said it best: "But let your 'Yes' be 'Yes,' and your 'No,' 'No.' For whatever is more than these is from the evil one" (Matthew 5:37, NKJV).

Followers have an inherent expectation that leaders will follow through with what they say.

Communication builds trust. Accurate, consistent, and open communication builds trust between leaders and followers and between leaders and leaders. It also reflects the measure of trust already present in an organization. Again, here is the irony: when trust is low, communication needs to be high. When trust is high, communication is not nearly as urgent. Yet this is exactly the time to communicate, because if you don't, you end up destroying the very trust you've worked so hard to build.

Trust is the primary asset of leadership. If people trust you, they will follow you. If they don't trust you, they will not follow you. Therefore, if you want more trust, and you want people to follow you, communicate accurately, consistently, and openly.

Competency #2: Creating Culture

Culture is not limited to the common practices and beliefs of an ethnicity or race. Any group of people who share a number of significant experiences over time develop assumptions about each other and the world around them. These assumptions begin as a set of consciously or subconsciously agreed-upon beliefs that gradually become accepted by the group. Edgar Schein explains:

> The term 'culture' should be reserved for the deeper level of basic assumptions and beliefs that are shared by members of an organization, that operate unconsciously, and that define in a basic 'taken for granted' fashion an organization's view of itself and its environment. These assumptions and beliefs are learned responses to a group's problems of survival in its external environment and its problems of internal integration.[35]

Inside a group, unspoken social creeds develop. These include how acceptance and belonging are gained, how conflict is resolved, and how status and power are achieved. Beliefs also form as a group exists in relationship to the external world. These beliefs have to do with how the group garners external resources in order to survive, how members view the world outside their own group, the assimilation of outsiders, and functions of mission and vision.

What begins as shared *beliefs* (assumptions) results in shared *values.* Values are those things that become uniquely esteemed by a group. They should be consciously chosen characteristics of a particular group that help them define themselves as unique in relation to other groups. Thus, they create a sense of shared identity among group members.

Ultimately, beliefs and values are expressed in *behavior.* In time, all three of these dimensions tend to operate subconsciously. They are taken for granted by the group and as such are no longer debated or discussed. This is the pinnacle of culture formation, which is a phenomenon that occurs in any group or organization—in churches, ethnic groups, work teams, sports teams, businesses, organizations, nations, and more.

The leadership skill of creating culture means that a leader *possesses an intentional understanding of the process of assumption formation* as well as competent ways to manage that process. Effective leaders understand how paradigms are formed within people and how mental maps (i.e. frameworks by which people see and interpret the world) are developed. In truth, we do not see the world as it is; we see it as we are. Therefore, in order to transform people in lasting ways, leaders must alter the lens by which people see the world—that is, they must affect the way people see themselves, God, and the world around them.

Leaders are God's primary instruments to create culture, direct it, sustain it, and when necessary, deconstruct it. Culture creation is an essential skill because culture dictates so many of a group's motivations and behaviors. Therefore, a leader should be clear about the assumptions that he or she believes are important, moral, and God-honoring for the group to possess—and about the assumptions they should reject. Since the formation of culture is the result of learned responses and conditioning, leaders do have the ability to form and transform culture.

Jesus knew how to speak to and change people's assumptions. As a leader, he challenged their paradigms, the things they valued, and their corrupt practices. He validated correct assumptions and sought to transform the ones inconsistent with the heart of God.

Jesus understood that the external practices he challenged (dietary laws, Sabbath keeping, purification rites, etc.) were connected to a deeper set of assumptions. They weren't just things that people did. Rather, the misguided application of the law practiced by people in his day was built upon errant paradigms about God and themselves in relation to him. In fact, their behaviors were more than just things they did. They were a part of their very identity—how they defined themselves as good and in relationship to God. Because of this, Jesus's life illustrates the limits of culture creation as well. As skilled as he was at speaking truth and challenging minds, there were many who just would not change deeply from within. These were the ones who ultimately rejected his message and truth.

While Jesus sought to change the hearts and minds of many, he also understood the value of starting from scratch. In the process of three years of teaching, leading, and doing life with twelve disciples, he was able to put "new wine into new wineskins" (Mark 2:22). These men, with the exception of one, took on a new belief system, and as a result a new culture was birthed. In time, empowered by the Holy Spirit of God, it would gain momentum and transform the world.

The Snowball Effect

Church leaders must understand the power of culture for both good and harm. Whether a particular culture is right and God-honoring or errant and destructive, the dynamic of culture itself provides a form of reinforcement that cements beliefs, values, and behaviors into the DNA of a group or organization. Culture can create a positive, upward spiral that leads to more positive and healthy characteristics or a negative, downward spiral that leads to more of the damaging and undesirable. Like a snowball rolling down a hill gets larger, faster, and more powerful, so culture increases its influence over time.

Of course, the goal for biblical leaders is not simply to create a culture within their organization, but to create a biblical and God-honoring one. This means that leaders must have a clear understanding of the kind of culture they seek to create, and it should be based upon God's Word. When from the Bible we discern the beliefs, values, and behaviors that represent a God-honoring, biblically-functioning community (such as is found in Acts 2:42–47, 1 Corinthians 12:12–30, and Ephesians 3:14–21), we can then go about being used by God to create that kind of community.

Diversity

A healthy culture means that a diverse group of people agrees about certain assumptions—not that they agree on all detailed applications of those assumptions. A healthy culture has room for difference in practice and uniqueness among its members. Culture in its extreme form is just *cult*—where everyone must look alike, act alike, speak alike, and think alike. God does not desire this for the church, nor is such a culture reflected in God's Word. The church should seek unity among its members, not uniformity.

How a Christian organization handles its beliefs is almost as important as the beliefs themselves. A powerful and healthy culture is formed when in essential beliefs there is unity and in nonessential beliefs there is diversity (see Romans 14). Churches get into trouble when they elevate nonessentials to the place of essentials. Subconscious and detailed codes of conduct are created, and no room is left for personal preference or opinion. In healthy churches, diversity in nonessentials (Paul would call these "disputable" or "interpretable" matters in Romans 14) is itself celebrated as an attribute of the culture. People in these churches feel that they belong and share an identity based upon a union in essentials, yet they also feel freedom as individuals to live out their own personal convictions. This balance reflects the very notion of the unity and diversity that Paul describes in the body of Christ in 1 Corinthians 12:12–31.

Jesus's disciples took on a new belief system,
and as a result a new culture was birthed—
one that would transform the world.

It is an important task for leaders to clarify for their people both what is essential and, by default, what is nonessential. Without defining essentials, the church lacks unity. Without allowing for nonessentials, the church lacks diversity.

Just as important as leaving room for diversity is the need for commitment to the essentials. For many healthy congregations (and other Christian organizations), these essentials include:

- Basic doctrinal beliefs. The leader must determine the answer to the question, "What essential doctrinal and theological beliefs must people subscribe to in order to be a part of this church?"
- Matters of vision and mission. Unity comes when people agree and commit themselves to the mission of the church (Matthew 28:18–20) and to its vision—the unique way the church will achieve that mission. "What convictions and agreement should people have about the *kind* of church we are?"

- Structure. Unity also comes when people have agreement about church polity and forms of leadership. "To what degree must congregants agree in advance with the way the church makes its decisions?"

In reality, many churches lack unity and build conflict into their cultures because they haven't clarified these essential matters. The same holds true for other Christian organizations.

Once the essentials are delineated, there is now greater understanding of the nonessentials. Everything outside the essentials is, of course, nonessential. There is room here for people's convictions, opinions, and preferential beliefs regarding "interpretable" matters of doctrine and specific applications of faith.

One other note: for those who aspire to leadership roles in the congregation or organization, qualifications should extend beyond just the essentials. In other words, it is fair and responsible to expect that leaders will have more doctrinal and ecclesiastical agreement than mere church members or volunteers.

An Invisible Force

Culture eventually takes on a life of its own. Once established, it has the potency to correct errant behavior as well as to reinforce what is right and good. This means that in the beginning of culture formation, the decisions a leader makes (or even chooses not to make) are of utmost importance. Leaders should make these early decisions carefully and faithfully. Why? Because these decisions set precedents for beliefs that the group will have in the future. In essence, they *teach* the group what to believe, what to value, and how to behave. Leaders do this by what they reward and punish, what they celebrate and lament, what they feed and starve, what they permit and do not permit, and what they talk about and remain silent about. In the early days, decisions are often challenged and debated, but later, with persistence and courage from the leader, culture gains traction.

When this happens, the potency level of the culture creates two valuable tools for the leader:

Labeling "saints and sinners." Culture expresses a positive reinforcement for those who act within it. Culture is an invisible force that reaffirms and supports people whose beliefs, values, and behaviors are consistent with it. These are people who will gain acceptance, status, and possibly power. These we might call "saints." By default, culture also spotlights those who act inconsistently with it. In effect, culture punishes beliefs, values, and behaviors that don't align with it. This serves a correcting role when "sinners" repent (i.e., come back into alignment with culture). When sinners don't repent, culture serves as a purging dynamic. In time, these people leave because the force of culture eventually expels them outward.

On its own, culture is an invisible force that rewards those who act congruently with it and defends against those who might seek to change it. This creates a positive dynamic for the leader as it allows the organization to correct itself without the leader's attention and energy and without the conflict that often comes with attempting to bring people back into alignment. However, this reality also stands as a bulwark against change and makes the job difficult for leaders seeking to transform already solidified cultures.

A wooing effect. Similarly, culture, within its own power, possesses a persuading force for those outside it. It has the ability to attract and entice. When obvious and compelling, a positive culture emits an inherent energy that will draw in those new to it or those who stand outside it. Churches notice this power at work when they move from numeric growth in the form of addition (one person/one family at a time) to growth in the form of multiplication (numerous people/families at a time). Growth becomes exponential due to the wooing effect of culture as used by the Holy Spirit. This dynamism becomes instilled into a group and compels others to join.

Early leadership decisions teach a group what to believe,
what to value, and how to behave.

Competency #3: Leading Change

Change is at the very heart of leadership. If you're not willing to embrace change, you're not ready to lead. Moreover, leaders cannot just tolerate change; they must be catalysts for it. God always has a future for us to pursue, and he seeks to use leaders to take people from their present state into his ideal future. JFK said it well: "Change is the law of life. And those who look only to the past or present are certain to miss the future."[36]

The Reason for Change

The centrality of change to effective leadership does not mean changing for change's sake. It doesn't mean chasing a church growth fad or revolutionizing a church service every week. The idea here is much broader. Within every change in a church or ministry, there is a spiritual question to be answered: *What does God want us to be?*

The answer to this question naturally leads a group to discover what God wants them to do in order to become what he desires. The ultimate reason for change is not that the world is in need. The ultimate reason for change is not that the church is ineffective. *The ultimate reason for change is that God is leading us to change.* If change is enacted for any other reason than this, that change has the potential to fail or to produce only temporary, worldly results.

Leaders should be convinced in their hearts that a particular change is being led by God, that it is a spiritual adventure, and that they should seek to guide others through the change experience in a way that ultimately yields more faith and Christlikeness than the group currently possesses. Leaders are called to be change agents for eternal purposes.

Leaders cannot just tolerate change; they must be catalysts for it.

God's New Thing

While God and the gospel never change, God's methods do. God is uniquely creative. He has displayed this quality throughout history He has chosen to do many different things in different ways, all with the purpose of revealing himself and redeeming mankind. Think about some of the creative methods of God: Joseph's dreams, the ten plagues, the Red Sea experience, manna in the wilderness, Gideon's fleece, Balaam's talking donkey, water into wine, the miraculous healings by Jesus and the apostles, the revelation of St. John—his creativity is endless!

There are two reasons God changes his methods. First, the world is always changing, and the needs of the moment therefore change. The effectiveness of a method will be different in different cultures and times and with different people, and God seems well aware of this. Second, as with our discussion on methodolatry, God wants to make sure we don't have faith in the *way* he does things as opposed to having faith in *him.* Believers can marry themselves to methods in such a way that they begin to have confidence in them. In this, they often seek to replicate the method so that the work of God might be repeated. Yet, doing so takes little faith. When we trust God beyond the methods of the past (even the good or miraculous ones), then we have eyes to see the new things he is doing and the new ways he wants to work. In essence, God keeps us guessing so that we will keep our eyes on him.

God is uniquely creative and has displayed
this quality for centuries.

Take, for example, Isaiah 43:16–21:

This is what the Lord says—
he who made a way through the sea,
a path through the mighty waters,

who drew out the chariots and horses,
the army and reinforcements together,
and they lay there, never to rise again,
extinguished, snuffed out like a wick:
"Forget the former things;
do not dwell on the past.
See, I am doing a new thing!
Now it springs up; do you not perceive it?
I am making a way in the wilderness
and streams in the wasteland.
The wild animals honor me,
the jackals and the owls,
because I provide water in the wilderness
and streams in the wasteland,
to give drink to my people, my chosen,
the people I formed for myself
that they may proclaim my praise.

Through the prophet Isaiah, God here reminds the remnant of the Jewish faithful in exile that he is doing something new. Yet, the way God's words are presented here is fascinating. The passage begins by qualifying who the Lord is. He is the One who "made a way through the sea," who "drew out the chariots" and "extinguished" them "never to rise again." This of course is a reference to the Red Sea experience under Moses's leadership. I can imagine the people in Isaiah's day—a remnant seeking to survive in their faith—saying to themselves, "If only we had a Moses again! If only God would work another Red Sea miracle!" But after describing this, the greatest miracle in the history of Israel, in the very next verse God says, "Forget the former things. Do not dwell on the past."

What? Forget about Moses? Forget about the Red Sea? God is saying that even this amazing miracle, with all the good it brought in the past, should not be dwelt upon in the sense that doing so would cause his people to want to repeat it or depend upon it. It's not just the bad things from the past that can keep us from God's future. It's the good things as well. This past-tense faith causes us to be blind to new things that God is doing: "See, I am doing a new thing! Now it springs up; do you not perceive it?"

What is that new thing? In v. 19 God says, "I am making a way in the wilderness and streams in the wasteland" and "I provide water in the wilderness." In the past, God provided *dry land in the water*. In the future, God will put *water in the dry land*. God will do in the future the exact opposite of what he did in the past! Consequently, for us there remains that convicting question from God: "Do you not see it or perceive it?"

Despite any method God seeks to use, leaders must be connected to the very heart of God to be sure that they are not trusting in a method from the past but rather in the God who worked through that method. We need leaders today who think outside of the framework of what has already been done. If leaders do this and effectively lead their people to do the same, change will become a faith adventure with eternal results. People won't change merely because of a need, a crisis, or a fad. They will change as an act of worship and obedience to the God whom they are following and trusting.

It's not just the bad things from the past
that can keep us from God's future.
It's the good things as well.

The Change Process

Leading change can be understood in three phases: insight, foresight, and oversight. The one constant in each phase is the word "sight," which refers to the dynamic of vision. *Vision for the future is the key characteristic and motivator in any major change endeavor.* Vision initiates change, is the driving force during change, and sustains change in the long term.

Nehemiah provides the greatest biblical example of this process in Scripture.

Insight refers to the *assessment* phase of change. It is expressed in Nehemiah 1:1–2:10. For Nehemiah, insight included these key elements:

- The report regarding the destroyed walls of Jerusalem (Nehemiah 1:1–3).
- Nehemiah's prayer of confession, reaffirmation of God's purposes, and request for God's intervention (Nehemiah 1:4–11).
- God's answer to Nehemiah's prayer. Through a divinely appointed discussion with Nehemiah, the king of Persia allowed Nehemiah to return to Jerusalem, guaranteeing safe passage and timber for the work. Nehemiah's immediate response to the king reveals that he had thought and planned enough to know what he needed to begin the project. He expected God to answer his prayer and planned accordingly.
- Nehemiah's inspection of the walls. He traveled with his entourage to Jerusalem and inspected the situation himself (Nehemiah 2:11–16). He did research and engaged in thoughtful consideration of the need, the scope of the project, and the way the work could be accomplished.

Before sharing the vision with others and before any physical labor on the walls began, Nehemiah went through extensive self-examination, assessment, requests for divine provision, and contemplation upon God and his purposes. While leaders often overlook the insight phase and rush to implementation, it indeed may be the most important of the three.

We can deduce several principles from Nehemiah's experience and from this first phase of the change process that apply today:

1. Assessing Reality. Max Depree said, "The first responsibility of a leader is to define reality."[37] The initial act of leading change is assessing exactly what the need is. Charles Kettering, the famous inventor and head of research for GM, said, "A problem well-stated is a problem half-solved."[38] Assessment should not be

underestimated or quickly overlooked. Leaders must consider not only the temporal, material needs at hand, but also the deeper spiritual implications. What is the need present in this situation? What does God want to do in and through this crisis or challenge?

Nehemiah heard the news of the broken walls, immediately entered into prayer because of it, and through prayer reaffirmed God's eternal purposes and promises that applied to this need. Beyond rebuilding physical walls, Nehemiah saw a spiritual need as well—to rebuild and restore the Jewish faith. As the walls would be rebuilt, so would their faith and encouragement.

For us today, using God's Word as a guide is the key to assessing current reality in light of God's purposes. What is God's eternal mission? What is the church's mission? What are the purposes the church should pursue? Biblical images and imperatives such as Matthew 28:18–20 and Acts 2:42–47 are of value here. We should compare current reality in the world to God's ideal in the Word.

2. Assessing Readiness. Sometimes change fails not because it's wrong, but because it's wrong timing. The leader and/or the church were not prepared and not ready. There was not yet a willingness or desire for change. Nehemiah prayed and waited on God. At the right time, under God's provision and in his timing, he acted with courage and faith—but not before.

This assumes that leaders (the change agents) are not always immediately ready for change and that the church or organization (the recipients of the change) may not immediately be ready for it. Both must be assessed.

Change always demands more of the leader than anyone else. Assessment here includes many personal questions. As the leader, am I ready for change and the emotional toll it may exact? Am I spiritually prepared in my heart and living in deep connection with God? Is this change about God's purposes or my aspirations? Am I willing to embrace the behaviors, beliefs, and sacrifices needed to lead this change? As I lead change, am I willing to change myself?

Leaders must also determine the degree of readiness among those being asked to change. They ask: "Is my church ready for change?" Of course, when there is apathy or indifference, leaders may be used to move a church and its people into desiring change. They may help create a sense of urgency by highlighting physical and spiritual needs as well as God's desire to meet those needs. They may communicate vision and a compelling picture of an ideal future. This creates an *appetite* for change by placing desires within people for a preferred future state. Leaders may preach and teach about God's eternal purposes, how those purposes apply to the people's context, and the benefits that change will bring as they seek to do God's will. All of these prepare a group for change.

3. Assessing Resources. Nehemiah personally went and carefully inspected Jerusalem and its condition. Even before he arrived, he had studied the situation and gained some sense of the resources necessary for the project. In other words, he did his homework. He came to understand through investigation and study what exactly was needed in his particular context.

For leaders today, this form of analysis is important. Understanding yourself, your church's people, your community, and your particular framework for change is vital. This might include researching demographics (family, marital status, age, ethnicity, etc.), analyzing financial trends, making numeric projections, and/or honestly assessing people's spiritual condition. Upon understanding these matters, leaders can then come to know what resources are necessary to meet needs as well as what prayers to pray in asking God to provide.

Foresight refers to the *communication* phase of change. Though this phase began with the introspective prayer of Nehemiah, it is principally expressed in Nehemiah 2:11–20.

- Nehemiah discerned vision (Nehemiah 1:4–11). There is no doubt that during his initial three–four month period of prayer and intro-spection, he sensed a calling from God. He began to realize that God wanted to use him to rebuild Jerusalem's walls and thereby restore a measure of faith to the Jewish people. We learn this because of Nehemiah's specific request toward the end of that period when he asked God to intervene in his meeting with the king: "Make your servant successful today and grant him compassion before this man" (Nehemiah 1:11). It was Nehemiah's prayer that God would work in such a way that he would gain permission and resources from the king to go and rebuild. It is obvious, therefore, that in his period of prayer and self-analysis, a calling was implanted in Nehemiah's heart, and with it a vision of a future, ideal state.
- Nehemiah communicated vision (Nehemiah 2:11–20). Up to this point, Nehemiah had mainly communicated with the king. At the proper time, Nehemiah expressed his calling and vision to others. He communicated it in four ways:
  - As an urgent need: "You see the bad situation we are in, that Jerusalem is desolate and its gates burned by fire" (v. 2:17a). He communicated his discontentment with the current situation. His goal was for others to sense the same discontent and see that this situation was unacceptable for the people of God. Nehemiah communicated urgency by allowing people to see the negative reality. It's interesting that he waited to share his vision until the people could arrive in Jerusalem and see the walls up close and personal. Talking about a need from a distance is one thing. Seeing the need up close provides a picture of the situation—and as is said, a picture paints a

thousand words. Nehemiah's choice to share the vision in the context of showing the need was a wise communication tool.

- With a clear and compelling vision statement: "Come, let us rebuild the wall of Jerusalem" (v. 2:17b). Based upon the situation and the need, here was his positive solution: "Let us rebuild the wall of Jerusalem." It was a clear call to action. Vision does not stay in the negative. Instead, it should always be expressed as a positive solution to a negative situation.
- For a spiritual result: ". . . so that we will no longer be a reproach" (v. 2:17c). Nehemiah connected the rebuilding of the physical walls of Jerusalem to the rebuilding of the spiritual walls of Israel. Jerusalem was the symbol of God's work and presence with his people. By rebuilding the city, the people would once again sense the firm foundation of their security and hope in Yahweh. Their faith would once again be restored.
- With a divine provision: "I told them how the hand of my God had been favorable to me and also about the king's words which he had spoken to me. Then they said, 'Let us arise and build'" (v. 2:18). In the context of communicating vision, Nehemiah also stated how God had already supernaturally provided for the vision. Telling the people about this miracle enthused them and jumpstarted action and courage within them so they could begin the work.

In the process of leading change, the *foresight* phase is all about the future work of God in and through the leader and his or her people. It is in this phase that the leader discerns God's vision and begins to communicate it. This vision, when stated clearly, concisely, and compellingly, and when based upon a clear calling of God, brings urgency, desire, hope, and willingness for people to change. Consequently, the power of vision to effect change cannot be overemphasized.

For people in leadership today, this means:

1. Leaders must carefully discern God's vision. Leaders need to gain as much clarity as possible about their calling and vision before sharing with others (see chapter 4, "Calling").

2. Leaders must own the vision themselves. The vision will never be achieved beyond the willingness and sacrifice of the leader. Vision does not stand outside a leader, but burns within him or her. There is a sense within leaders that this vision *must* take place. It is the right and godly thing to do, and all effort and energy must be brought to bear upon enacting the positive solution to a negative situation. Leaders own the burden first and foremost. It flows out of them to the people they lead. With regards to communicating to others, *vision is not taught by the leader, but caught from the leader.*

3. Leaders should communicate vision with clarity and simplicity. Sometimes leaders communicate vision in complex and lengthy ways. Visions should be stated succinctly and unambiguously. If vision statements are not brief enough to be memorized, they lose their power. Ultimately, a leader should arrive at a clear, concise, and compelling vision statement that, at the right time, can be shared with others. Nehemiah's vision statement was succinct: "Come, let us rebuild the wall of Jerusalem."

4. The spiritual benefits of the vision will create desire. When spiritual results are attached to a vision, people are much more willing to sacrifice for it. People see a vision's importance when eternity and spiritual need is clearly at stake and when the benefits of achieving the vision outweigh the work involved.

5. God's activity surrounding the vision must be communicated. If the vision is indeed from God, and if leaders have prayed for God's hand to work in and through the vision, there should be some evidence of divine activity and provision regarding it. Leaders must have eyes to see God working, and in the context of sharing vision, they should communicate to others God's supernatural activity. This brings enthusiasm and validates the fact that God has ordained the work.

Oversight refers to the *implementation* phase of change. This is the roll-out phase, and it requires good planning, management, and determination. The next lengthy portion of the book of Nehemiah (2:19 through chapter 6) illustrates Nehemiah's superb execution of the change project. Chapters 7–9 describe the response of the people after the walls were rebuilt.

Here are some characteristics of the implementation phase:

- Immediate opposition (Nehemiah 2:19–20). The first recorded event after the decision to start this work was opposition. Neighboring factions from outside Nehemiah's camp, led by Sanballat the Horonite, Tobiah the Ammonite, and Geshem the Arab, mocked and despised their work. Nehemiah stood firm—not on his own strength, but on the conviction that "the God of heaven will give us success" (v. 2:20).
- Structure and organization (Nehemiah 3). Work was well organized and divided among families. Each family unit had a clear responsibility and was empowered to make the necessary repairs to an assigned gate and its accompanying section of the wall. There was a high sense of ownership, empowerment and cooperation among the people.
- More opposition (Nehemiah 4:1–7). The same cast of characters returned with intensified opposition. They ridiculed the laboring people by questioning their motivations (Nehemiah 4:2) and by minimizing the quality and strength of their work: "Even what they are building—if a fox should jump on it, he would break their stone wall down!" (Nehemiah 4:3).
- Discouragement overcome (Nehemiah 4:9–23). The discouragement and fear caused by the opposition was conquered through prayer and the visionary leadership of Nehemiah. Throughout the project, the people had a deep dependence upon God through prayer (v. 4:9), Nehemiah's encouragement as leader (v. 4:14), the vision before them of the restored walls (v. 4:15), and Nehemiah's

intelligent structuring of the project that would ensure their productivity and safety (vv. 4:16–23).

- Alignment and integrity (Nehemiah 5:1–13). The Jewish nobles and rulers in Jerusalem were taxing the commoners as they did the work on the walls. This led to division within the city and an outcry from people regarding these abuses. Nehemiah was indignant that these leaders would do such a thing. He called them together and explained how this act was enslaving their Jewish brothers just as the conquering nations had done. He entreated them to give back the vineyards, houses, and money they had exacted from the commoners. These leaders saw the error of their ways and heartily agreed to do as Nehemiah had petitioned.

- Godly example (Nehemiah 5:14–19). Nehemiah tells us that from the onset of the project, he as governor did not take the royal food allowance as he was entitled to do. The former governors did so and thereby placed burdens on the people. By contrast, Nehemiah shared his large food allotment with others. Additionally, he himself worked as a laborer on the wall.

- A final attempt to distract (Nehemiah 6:1–14). Sanballat, Tobiah, and Geshem tried one more time to thwart the work of the project. They invited Nehemiah to a meeting in order to ambush him. Nehemiah saw through their plot and responded, "I am doing a great work and I cannot come down" (v. 6:3). They attempted this four times, and each time Nehemiah replied the same way. Sanballat then sought to frighten Nehemiah by questioning his motivations for the work, saying that it was being done for the purpose of gaining power to rebel against Persia. While he feared the king might hear this rumor and actually believe it, Nehemiah ignored the lie and prayed for God to strengthen his hands (v. 6:9). Finally, these three enemies hired someone from within Jerusalem to frighten Nehemiah with a threat to his life. The Jew Shemaiah entreated Nehemiah to hide in the temple in order to take cover from the danger. Once again, this was an attempt to dissuade him away from the work. Nehemiah perceived the deception and prayed that God would remember Sanballat, Tobiah, and Geshem according to their evil works—as well as any prophets in Jerusalem who were trying to frighten him (v. 6:14).

- Completion of the project (Nehemiah 6:15–19). The walls and gates surrounding the city were restored with amazing efficiency—in only fifty-two days! Nehemiah had remained focused and kept his faith until the end of the project.

- Census, celebration, confession, and covenant (Nehemiah 7–9). Now that the project was complete and the change process ending, there was a time for rest and reflection. A census was taken for historical purposes. The people celebrated their achievement by doing what was fitting—giving God glory! They did this by having Ezra read the law before the people, marking the day as holy and sacred, and restoring the Feast of Booths, which commemorated Israel's rescue from Egypt and their days before Jerusalem was given to them. The book of Nehemiah ends with a long confession of the people's sins against God and their vow to follow the Lord in the future. They documented this covenant in writing, with the names of the leaders, Levites, and priests affixed to it.

There is much to learn from Nehemiah in the *oversight* phase of change.

1. Change will face opposition—count on it. Satan always attempts to thwart God-honoring change from the very beginning. Savvy leaders understand this and are not surprised or thrown off when it comes. We must have the same disposition as the apostle Paul when he wrote, ". . . in order that Satan might not outwit us. For we are not unaware of his schemes" (2 Corinthians 2:11). At times, this opposition will come from outsiders: in the form of criticism, questions about our character, or challenges to our motivations. At other times, opposition will come from within. This is often the most disheartening form of opposition because it involves

rejection and possible betrayal from those who are a part of the work.

2. We resist opposition through strength of calling, prayer, and integrity. Nehemiah's strength and stability came as a result of the surety of his call to go and rebuild Jerusalem's walls. When you are sure that God has called you and provided vision, you have the ability to withstand hardship. *In truth, there is a correlation between courage and calling.* Beyond this, throughout the entire book of Nehemiah, we see a pattern of constant, prayerful dependence upon God. If you study these prayers, you will see that these requests were for emotional strength and a spirit of endurance as Nehemiah laid the opposition at God's feet for him to deal with.

3. Change must be organized and well structured. Sometimes change endeavors implode because they lack planning and/or are implemented poorly. One huge lesson we learn from Nehemiah is that a well-structured change project has the ability in itself to enthuse and empower. This means:

   • Clear instructions for the work to be done and who will do it.
   • A project timeline and structure that is laid out in an organized fashion.
   • People given the resources and tools they need for the work.

4. Leaders remove distractions and protect their people from opposition. A big role of leaders during change is to protect their people from threats to their emotional stability as well as to the actual work project. In this sense, leaders run interference for their people and handle the uglier matters that stand outside or against the change process. Leaders thus free their people to focus on the most important tasks at hand.

5. Leaders respond to dire moments with courage and faith. When people lose heart, leaders believe. They believe that the work is

worthwhile; they believe it is from God; they believe it will be accomplished. Sometimes the only way to keep change alive is for a leader to rise up when he or she sees discouragement in others and provide them audacious words of hope and courage.

When I saw their fear, I rose and spoke to the nobles, the officials and the rest of the people: "Do not be afraid of them; remember the Lord who is great and awesome, and fight for your brothers, your sons, your daughters, your wives and your houses. (Nehemiah 4:14, emphasis mine)

6. Leaders align all elements of the organization with the change. In Nehemiah 5, when the nobles acted in ways inconsistent with the moral character of the change Nehemiah was leading, he became angry. It appalled him that in this noble work, leaders would act so dishonorably. The lesson here is that there are no exceptions. Not only must the change be moral and God-honoring, so also must the people and the process along the way. If there are exceptions, then the entire change endeavor can unravel as it loses credibility.

7. During change, leaders do not demand of others what they are unwilling to give themselves. Nehemiah provides an ideal model of servant leadership when he refused a privilege of his powerful position and instead shared his royal food allotment with others. He also spent time laboring alongside people on the wall. By doing such acts, leaders illustrate their willingness to do as others are asked to do. This brings credibility to the leader and trust in the change endeavor.

8. Leaders stay the course and do not give up. Many things can distract and cause mission drift. Good leaders stay focused upon the task at hand and measure their activity in terms of how it contributes to the change project as a whole. Diversions caused by opposition, weariness, and busyness, as well as the standard demands

of a lengthy project, do not dissuade the leader from the end goal. Leaders finish what they begin.

9. At the end of the change process, it is right to stop and give glory to God. It was God who began the change in Nehemiah when he wept and prayed; it was God who supernaturally resourced the process; and it was God who sustained it and brought it to completion. This principle implies two things: (1) There should always be a finish line to the change process. In other words, change should never be ongoing and constant. People cannot handle perpetual change. Rather, with each change endeavor, there should be a start line and a finish line. Lead people from a point of origin to a point of clear destination. Then, if God leads, after rest and celebration, a new change adventure may begin. (2) It is fitting, once change has been achieved, that a glorious gathering of God's people take place for the purpose of ascribing worship to God. As Andy Stanley rightly says, "The end of a God-ordained vision is God."[39]

Insight, foresight, and *oversight.* Each phase plays a key role in the change process. **Insight** assesses vision by focusing on the need and defining current reality as well as the exact challenge at hand, always in light of God's purpose and promises. **Foresight** communicates vision, thereby providing a stirring desire for a positive future state. **Oversight** implements vision through the management and structure of the project, ensuring that people who begin the change process will be successful in the end. All three of these phases speak to basic facets about change within people: People change when they *hurt* enough that they *have to* change (current reality); when they *hope* enough that they *want to* change (vision of the future); and when they *have* enough that they *can* change (structure and resources).[40]

Competency #4: Resolving Conflict

Some go into ministry romanticizing what it will be like. They imagine that everyone will always get along and that people will love every leadership decision they make. This myth is propagated by the notion that "Things will be different in my church." The rude awakening is that every church or Christian organization has its share of conflict.

In fact, for various reasons, conflict can be more prevalent and complicated in the church than outside of it. The reasons for this are positive in one sense, but they can have negative side effects.

Three reasons in particular are significant:

1. Volunteers. The church is a magnificent volunteer organization where most people freely give of themselves to the work of ministry. However, since volunteers are unpaid, leaders don't have the same leverage for decision-making and dealing with conflict as those who supervise and lead in environments where people are compensated. People more quickly line up with leaders who have the ability to reward or punish them financially (salary, benefits, etc.). Church leadership, on the other hand, requires a completely different set of influencing skills in order to gain acceptance for major decisions and to deal with conflict when there is disagreement.

2. "My opinion matters." Because we work with volunteers, and these people give willingly in support of the church, many of them feel they have the right to voice their opinion and be heard. Of course, they're right—provided that the way they express their opinion lines up with God's Word (Ephesians 4:15). When channeled correctly, people's feeling the freedom to voice feedback is a good thing. It reflects a high sense of ownership and concern among the church family. Yet, this creates a challenge when there is a large quantity of concerned and opinionated people and when what one person would like to see take place differs from the preference of another. In the church, as opposed to a paid work environment, opinions are often more outspoken because ownership and loving concern for the church is higher.

Leaders must create legitimate and safe channels
for people to express concerns and questions.

---

3. Everyone can do your job. Many people in the church feel that they are as much an expert on ministry as the leader is. People often don't consider the experiences and training pastors and ministry leaders have had, nor are they aware of the sensitivities involved in how decisions must be made. This reality often rubs church leaders the wrong way. Therefore, leaders must find a means of remaining humble enough to listen, at times, to inexperienced and uniformed people. This does not mean that the pastor alone must entertain every opinion of every person who has one. Still, leaders must create legitimate and safe channels for people to express concerns and questions.

Regardless of the reasons that it happens in ministry, conflict must be responded to in effective and emotionally stable ways. Healthy conflict responses are built upon several key truths that leaders should accept:

1. Conflict is normal. Churches are filled with sin-stained and emotionally needy people who are different from one another in personality and perspective. These traits are also true of the church's leaders. This therefore means that conflict will occur. Conflict among Christians has happened from the beginning of Christianity (Luke 9:46, Acts 15, 1 Corinthians 3:1–8), and it is good for leaders to normalize it to a degree and accept it as a fact of church life.

2. Conflict is healthy. Conflict is actually a sign of health. It means that people are talking deeply and caring deeply about things. A total lack of disagreement would indicate a low sense of ownership and burden about the church. In truth, there are many dying

churches that experience no conflict. This is often because people are fearful to share their thoughts and feelings or to proactively express a concern. The leader might be unwilling to listen and callous in attitude. It might also indicate that people just don't care much about the welfare and success of the church. As a sign of health, unquestioned uniformity and indifference are much worse than a small degree of conflict.

3. Conflict is creative. Conflict, handled biblically, often gives birth to positive things. It is not only creative in that it leads to solutions, but it has the potential to bring about oneness between people through the process of problem-solving and conflict resolution. When conflict is managed properly, people will be closer to one another afterward than they were before. *Said another way, churches will not be as unified without conflict as they can be with it.* Remember, tolerance is not the same as unity. Tolerance means that people are putting up with one another. It is a passive and reactive reality that, while important (Ephesians 4:2–3), does not achieve God's very best for the church. The Lord wants us to do more than tolerate each other. His desire is that we be unified in heart and purpose (John 17). Unity is an active, affirming reality where people who are different come together to join hearts and hands in the great mission of God. Tolerance is surviving. Unity gives life. The process of conflict resolution, as opposed to experiencing no conflict at all, has the potential to bring unity and vibrancy to a congregation.

Conflict means that people are talking deeply
and caring deeply about things.
It can be a sign of health.

The Process and Principles of Conflict Resolution

The Scripture gives clear principles and processes for conflict resolution. These are essential to effective biblical leadership and empower the leader to face the difficult and often complex matter of conflict with deep confidence.

> You have heard that it was said to those of old, "You shall not murder; and whoever murders will be liable to judgment." But I say to you that everyone who is angry with his brother will be liable to judgment; whoever insults his brother will be liable to the council; and whoever says, "You fool!" will be liable to the hell of fire. So if you are offering your gift at the altar and there remember that your brother has something against you, leave your gift there before the altar and go. First be reconciled to your brother, and then come and offer your gift. (Matthew 5:21–24)

> If your brother sins against you, go and tell him his fault, between you and him alone. If he listens to you, you have gained your brother. But if he does not listen, take one or two others along with you, that every charge may be established by the evidence of two or three witnesses. If he refuses to listen to them, tell it to the church. And if he refuses to listen even to the church, let him be to you as a Gentile and a tax collector. Truly, I say to you, whatever you bind on earth shall be bound in heaven, and whatever you loose on earth shall be loosed in heaven. Again I say to you, if two of you agree on earth about anything they ask, it will be done for them by my Father in heaven. For where two or three are gathered in my name, there am I among them. (Matthew 18:15–20)

1. The Clear Process

The first thing that must be recognized in these passages is that interpersonal relationships and the resolution of conflict are of supreme importance to God. In the Matthew 5 passage, Jesus envisions worshippers who worship in harmony with one another. Here in his first public sermon, he introduces the radical notion that true worship is not only about our vertical relationship with the Father, but also about our horizontal relationship with one another. Jesus taught that our relationship with God is hindered when our relationship with others is broken (see Matthew 6:15, 1 John 4:20, 1 Peter 3:7). Even in the context of the propriety that accompanied Jewish worship in the temple, Jesus encouraged people to interrupt their worship activities in order to go and make a relationship right with another. It's obvious that reconciliation is valued by God more than religious ritual.

The same idea is found in the Matthew 18 text. One may deduce the supreme importance in God's economy for his followers to make relationships right by the explicit process that Jesus outlines for resolving conflict (vv. 15–17), the binding nature and divine affirmation surrounding the process's outcomes when done correctly (v. 18), and the pleasure of God associated with reconciliation as evidenced by the powerful presence of Christ himself within these efforts (v. 20).

Though similar in many respects, there are some differences in these passages worth pointing out. In Matthew 5, the worshipper recognizes he has offended someone in some way. The believer here is the *offender*. In Matthew 18, the believer is the *one offended* by another. The "offense" in Matthew 5 seems to include even a minor offense—"and there remember that your brother has something against you" (v. 23)—the idea being that even if the offense is not serious by measure, if it causes someone to have a grudge against you, you as the concerned, mature believer should go and make it right. In Matthew 18, the offense is serious: "If your brother sins against you" (v. 15). The word "sins" denotes the gravity of the offense. The idea here in Matthew 18 is that we should initiate Jesus's reconciliation process when there has been sin against us. (We may presume that Jesus does not encourage this process in the case of minor offenses or oversensitivity.) In both passages, whether one has offended or been sinned against, the believer is not to wait for the other person to come, but instead should immediately go and initiate the restoration of the relationship.

> Interpersonal relationships and the resolution of conflict
> are of supreme importance to God.

The process in Matthew 18 is explicit and therefore encouraging. If leaders would challenge their congregations and hold them accountable to employ this process, if they would model it in their own actions when rifts occur between them and others, and if they would teach and preach the power of hearts right with one another in the body of Christ, these leaders would find unity in their congregations and relief from the stresses of constant conflict in the church body.

There are four steps involved in Jesus's reconciliation process in Matthew 18:15–20:

Step 1: Go in private. Jesus clearly explained that the first step to resolving conflict is to go privately to the one with whom you have an offense and seek to restore the relationship. Here, believers explain to one another the wrongdoing and its consequences—"go and tell him his fault" (v. 15)—and offer to give and receive forgiveness. The goal is not to blame or to win the argument, but to "gain your brother" (v. 15).

Since Jesus says we must *first* go in private, this means that no other step in the process should come before this one. Indeed, the first thing to do is the best and most effective thing to do. Why? Because this first principle holds the potential to preempt all the other steps. If leaders and those in Christian organizations would simply follow this one clear point of order, two-thirds of conflicts they now encounter could go away.

The benefits to practicing this difficult yet simple action are twofold for church leaders: (1) conflict is resolved quickly (conflict intensifies the longer it lingers), and (2) conflict is resolved privately (conflict intensifies when more people are involved). Consequently, this first step offers the most protection to the church's unity, and leaders should have a strong commitment to see it practiced.

There are two unique applications of this text that I have personally practiced:

First, when people come to me as a leader with an offense or a problem they have with someone in the church, my initial question is, "Have you gone to and spoken to this person who offended you?" Many times the answer is no. My response is simple: "By the clear teaching of Scripture, I cannot entertain conversations about someone else until you have gone to that person first yourself." If they are willing to go, I instruct them on the attitudes necessary for the mature believer in resolving conflict, and we pray together for their meeting. If they are unwilling to go and speak to the other in private, I admonish them of the importance in God's eyes of doing this and try to help them envision the positive possibilities and benefits of the encounter. If they are still unwilling, I pray with them and move on in my heart without engaging this conflict again—unless it becomes more serious and more widely known (see the principles below). In obedience to Christ, my first obligation is to make sure that we as a church follow Jesus's unambiguous plan.

Second, when conflict develops toward me (or in me toward others), I apply this principle in a rather literal way. Sometimes I will receive an e-mail noting how I have offended someone. I have learned the hard way not to resolve conflict via e-mail. Typed text is often misunderstood because people assign meaning and emphasis to words in a way the writer never intended. People are also much more courageous behind a keyboard and will type things they would never say face-to-face. Typed words are permanent—and we shouldn't do anything permanently stupid because we are temporarily upset.

Likewise, telephone calls are not best for the purpose of resolving conflict. People cannot see facial expressions when speaking on the phone, and sometimes meaning is misunderstood. Therefore, when I receive such an e-mail, a "jab" in the hallway at church, or a voice message communicating offense, I have a simple and short reply: "Let's please get together face-to-face to discuss this."

I have often been amazed by the transformation in people when I request this. Many apologize and say it was not that big a deal after all, or that they were just having a bad day. Some say they do not want to convene a meeting and continue their rant—and if they are unwilling to meet, I simply delete their e-mail without reading it in its entirety. Some I never hear from again. And some actually come in to discuss the matter. The kinder, gentler version of the person usually shows up, and more times than not, matters are settled in a godly, restoring kind of way.

In obedience to Christ, my first obligation is to make sure
that we as a church follow Jesus's unambiguous plan.

Step 2: Take one or two with you. If after a private encounter the conflict is not resolved, believers should take one or two others who may help as objective third-party facilitators (v. 16). This is not to "gang up" or accuse, but rather to clearly identify fault and to use the counsel of witnesses to impartially discuss the validity of a charge. They may be able to verify what was actually done, as well as the weight of the offense, and they can observe what is said in the conversation and how it is said. In this sense, this step provides protection from false accusations to both the offended and the offender. These "one or two" might include a staff person from the particular area of ministry impacted, a spiritual leader respected by both parties, or even a Christian counselor who can provide wisdom and spiritual insight.

Step 3: Tell it to the church. Since Jesus is advocating an escalating process that includes more people only as the conflict continues to exist, it is appropriate to assume that he would encourage the "need to know" nature of this process to continue even at this third level. In other words, when Jesus says "tell it to the church" (v. 17), he is not necessarily advocating a public gathering of the entire congregation. The idea is that church leadership should be involved at this point due to the possibility and necessity of formal church discipline taking place. These leaders may then determine the degree to which the congregation should be informed, making this judgment based upon the seriousness of the offense and the level of threat to church unity. Here church leaders and/or elders may act as facilitators, giving more serious guidance to the resolution than could be done in private or with other third parties, or if unsuccessful in that, they may move on to the next level in the process of resolving conflict as prescribed in verse 17.

Step 4: Cut off the unrepentant. Just as a commitment to restoring relationships is important to the health of a congregation, so also is the commitment of church leaders to protect God's flock from harmful people. After great strides are made to resolve conflict in the body, there is clear teaching here from Jesus in how to handle one who is unwilling and unrepentant. This assumes that there *are* such people in the world. In reality, there are people who actually do not want conflict resolved and who are unwilling to make peace. Leaders must not be so naïve as to think that there will never be people who, whether willfully or subconsciously, will attack and hurt a church family if left unchecked. Such folks should be dealt with shrewdly and always with the motivation to protect God's church. Sometimes, one of the functions of a biblical leader is to show people the metaphorical back door. Here, although restoration has not taken place, the conflict has been resolved and dealt with conclusively. Leaders must understand that while reconciliation is the goal, it does not always occur. Consequently, resolving a conflict is not always the same as reconciliation and does not always include restoration. It is resolved, but without reconciliation. This form of resolution is consistent with other New Testament teachings regarding the handling of the unrepentant (see Romans 16:17–18, 1 Corinthians 5:1–13, Titus 3:9–11, 2 Thessalonians 3:13–15).

When Jesus said regarding the unrepentant, "Let him be to you as a Gentile and a tax collector" (v. 17), the wording is important. The idea is to treat them as *you*—the Jewish people of his day—would a Gentile and tax collector. Jesus certainly befriended such people and encouraged love toward them as outsiders. But he knew how his audience looked upon Gentiles and tax collectors, and using the way they isolated themselves from such people as an example, he instructs the church to separate from the unrepentant believer.

The Process Results: Confidence and Christ's Presence

Jesus instills great confidence in those who walk through the conflict resolution process by assuring them that when it is practiced as he prescribes, all outcomes can be trusted to the Lord (vv. 18–19). Whatever is decided by the church regarding believers and their conflict is connected to heavenly authority and approval: "Whatever you bind on earth shall be bound in heaven, and whatever you loose on earth shall be loosed in heaven" (v. 18). If a repentant one is restored, that one's restoration is sealed in heaven as well. If one is unrepentant and thus expelled, heaven affirms such decisions—provided, of course, that this progression has taken place with the goal of forgiveness and redemption.

Moreover, when Jesus's process is followed, Christ promises his presence in and through it. Verse 20 is often quoted as a promise regarding prayer: "For where two or three are gathered in my name, there am I among them." However, the biblical context reveals that the promise relates to conflict resolution. Through his Holy Spirit, Christ is powerfully present when believers meet together for the purpose of making relationships right! When his followers meet to exchange forgiveness and pray together for reconciliation, Christ is "all in" these kinds of encounters. His heart remains close to those who follow his clear instructions to restore relationships, and even when such meetings do not produce reconciliation, leaders can walk away fully assured that what was decided on earth is affirmed in heaven and that God is in the midst of their efforts.

When Jesus's process is followed,
Christ promises his presence in and through it.

Leaders who trust God's Word by applying the resolution process Jesus outlined in Matthew 18 will see several benefits:

1. *Christ is honored.* When we do what Jesus told us to do, he is honored, and we have placed ourselves and our church in a context for his blessing and favor.
2. *It works.* This process allows for the greatest possibility of reconciliation and restoration between God's people as well as the greatest protection for the church.
3. *It protects the leader.* Leaders who practice Jesus's process will find that over time, people learn what to expect. Word will spread that those who come to the leader with an offense will be turned back and admonished to go and face the one who has offended them. They will also learn that if the offense is actually with the leader, a face-to-face meeting will be requested. Most people want to vent, but they want to do it from a distance. They often do not desire reconciliation as much as a platform to express frustration. As such, a commitment to Jesus's process will keep many conflicts away from a leader's door. When they do occur, the leader will have dealt with them the way conflict should and must be dealt with according to God's Word. Regardless of whether the process ends with reconciliation, the leader will have honored Christ by doing what he clearly taught. Even in those rare instances when the Matthew 18 process does not end well (Jesus never guaranteed that it would), the leader can walk away with integrity intact, knowing that he or she has acted in obedience to God.

4. *It builds healthy culture.* When leaders point people toward one another and model the Matthew 18 process in their own conflicts, the result is a church or organization that is conditioned to handle conflict in God-honoring ways. Culture is formed, and the positive spiral of unity and grace becomes implanted in the DNA of the group. In this sense, leaders will structure the group away from conflict rather than "feeding the monster." They teach the church the value of following God's Word and allow their people to experience the benefits of walking through conflict in a healthy way.

When these practices are in place, conflict becomes life-giving. Life-giving conflict is redeemable—fixable. It has the potential to give rise to creative solutions, build unity, and bring more power to a church or organization and its people. Life-giving conflict takes place when people who are offended find the maturity and emotional security to sit down together and resolve the problem under a leader's guidance.

In healthy organizations, people meet together to work things out due to a strong sense of the need to protect the unity of the group. This sense is imparted by leaders who teach about the importance of protecting unity; communicate the positive power and vision of a loving, unified Christian community; and model healthy conflict resolution to the rest of the body. Here, people sit down with one another because "our unity is more important than our differences." Commitment to unity leads to difficult and sometimes tearful conversations, yet always with the theme of redemption and restoration through the dialogue. "Making it right for the sake of the body and to the glory of God" is the overriding passion and goal.

Commitment to unity always prioritizes
redemption and restoration.

Strategies for a Leader's Response to Conflict

One of the overriding principles from Matthew 18 is that levels of conflict exist. In other words, not all conflict is the same. Some conflict threatens the life of the church—that is, the unity and health of the church family is at risk. Other conflicts are mild or moderate in their intensity and level of potential harm. Since this is true, not all conflict should be dealt with in the same manner. In fact, some conflict should not be dealt with at all *by leaders*. Categorizing the type of conflict faced provides a strategy for leaders in how to deal with it.

One way that conflict may be categorized is by understanding its scale and scope (or its intensity and impact, if you will). *Scale* has to do with the seriousness of the offense. *Scope* has to do with the number of people touched by the conflict. Matthew 18 teaches that a conflict's level of intensity is often related to the impact upon the number of people involved. That which starts out as a matter for two people to resolve between themselves can escalate all the way to the involvement of church leadership. Thus, the conflict's intensity increases. In reality, conflict that is not of a serious spiritual, theological, or moral *scale* and influences only one or two people in its *scope* requires a completely different response strategy than conflict that impacts many people and is weighty in its offense. Leaders should seek to limit the scope of conflict as much as possible to contain its impact upon an organization.

The resolution of conflict as Jesus outlined in Matthew 18 is an escalating process. The passage communicates the idea that people must first get together face-to-face to resolve their differences. Here, church leaders are not involved—which means that in a biblical model, leaders do not immediately jump into every conflict. Only when the intensity and impact of the conflict increases do leaders engage ("If he refuses to listen to them, tell it to the church" v. 17).

Applying the escalating principle from this passage, we are able to chart possible leader responses based upon intensity and impact. This is not an exact science; rather, this chart is given to allow leaders a way of categorizing conflict in a manner that helps them know how to deal with it at each level.

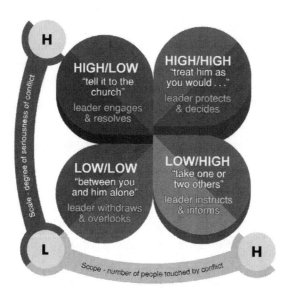

1. **Low/Low (low scale, low scope).** When conflict occurs between others and has little seriousness in terms of its spiritual, theological, or moral makeup, and when it touches only a handful of people, leaders should withdraw and overlook it. Low-scale and low-scope conflict results from personality differences, preferences in nonessentials of faith and practice, or disagreements about minor matters. Sometimes people will bring low-intensity and low-impact conflict to a leader. When a matter does not directly involve the leader, he or she should not entertain it, but should instead empower people to turn to one another privately and resolve it themselves. "If your brother sins against you, go and tell him his fault, between you and him alone" (Matthew 18:15). The leader should simply disregard this form of mild conflict. It will neither help the church to engage it nor hurt the church to ignore it. In truth, engaging this level of conflict could possibly harm the church, because when a leader gets involved

it feeds the conflict, enables high-maintenance people, and elevates the issue's seriousness unnecessarily. Leaders simply do not have the time or the emotional bandwidth to engage conflict at this level. This response is consistent with Jethro's advice to Moses about judging disputes among the Hebrews (see Exodus 18:17-23)

2. **Low/High (low scale, high scope).** When conflict is minor in its scale—its weight and intensity—but many have been touched by it or know about it, leaders should act as teachers to instruct and inform others in how to respond to it and resolve it. This is a great opportunity for empowerment and teaching about how the church should respond to one another when problems occur. Here the *primary* leader is still disengaged in terms of active involvement. Yet, he or she delegates responsibility to a staff member or layperson about how the conflict can be quickly settled: "take one or two others along with you" (Matthew 18:16). Depending upon the size of the church, the leader may not even be aware of the situation, provided that proactive training has occurred with others in how to handle conflict.

3. **High/Low (high scale, low scope).** When conflict is significant in scale, having moral, spiritual, or theological importance, leaders must engage and resolve it even when the number of people touched or informed about it is low. It is the seriousness of the offense that calls for a leader's involvement. Ignoring it sends inappropriate messages about the degree of its seriousness and abandons the leader's responsibility to protect the church from immorality, slander, or heresy. To protect the church, the leader should deal with the conflict *in private,* dealing only with those involved in the offense and those who have been directly impacted by it. In this situation, a leader may sit down with the offender and the offended in order to bring them together to make things right. The goal, as always, is to restore. In the event of a serious moral

failure, willful disregard of others, and/or lack of repentance, leaders may need to expel the offender from the congregation or terminate him or her from a staff position (Matthew 18:17, 1 Corinthians 5:1–12). This is dependent upon the degree of seriousness of the offense and the response of the offender. In some cases, reconciliation may happen but the consequences of an action still call for removal. This is particularly true of those in leadership. Leaders may disqualify themselves from positions of leadership for a period of time. If one in leadership is repentant and yet still needs to step down, the church should seek to support them with counseling, mentoring, care or financial resources. The goal remains their restoration. Of course, the wise counsel of other key leaders in the church would be beneficial in this decision.

4. **High/High (high scale, high scope).** This is the most serious of conflicts, significant both in scale and in scope. This is where conflict is public and severe. The general rule of thumb regarding conflict at any level is that leaders must engage it *when the unity of the church is threatened*. High scale and high scope conflict has the greatest potential to harm a congregation. A leader here must act as one who directs the conversation appropriately and decides what must be done; otherwise the church as a whole could be harmed. Here, the leader has a great opportunity to direct a group or even the entire church to experience "all things working together for good" (Romans 8:28). This is also the moment a leader must rise with courage to protect the church from harmful people—"And if he refuses to listen even to the church, let him be to you as a Gentile and a tax collector" (Matthew 18:17). The leader can display a calming presence and a prayerful spirit and yet a determined protection of the church. This teaches the group how to deal with disappointment or threat, exemplifies healthy leadership (providing more credibility to those in leadership), and has the potential to unify all those impacted by the conflict.

Other Principles of Conflict Resolution

1. Conflict Reveals Character. Conflict is often the mirror God uses to show us areas of needed character growth. *It may indeed be the primary way.* Through conflict, the strength of character—or lack thereof—within a leader is unveiled. God uses conflict to shine light upon our deepest motivations, our level of inner security, and the degree of integrity in our leadership. This is why biblical leaders must assimilate the character of Christ into the fabric of their everyday leadership. Only through the firm foundation of inner security, deepest integrity, and confident servanthood may leaders find the inner strength to endure these encounters.

2. Keep Conflict "Out There." Conflict associated with ministry requires secure emotional boundaries on the part of the leader. That's because leaders often mistakenly associate conflict with personal threat, professional failure, or the fear of being proven wrong or inadequate. Certainly conflict teaches us about ourselves, but if not seen objectively or processed properly, it can generate defeatism and self-condemnation.

Jesus possessed such inner security that he could emotionally withstand the personal attacks of others and yet still emotionally give himself to those in need. How is it that, with such virulent criticisms and verbal assaults coming his way, Jesus did not recoil into emotional isolation? His amazing sense of security came from knowing deep within who he was, from possessing integrity in what he did, and from the depth of intimacy in his relationship with the Father (John 13:3–5, John 17). These provided an inner fuel by which he could live for an audience of One, unconditionally love others who were in need, and grow intimate with those closest to him, and yet still protect his heart from collapse when conflict arose.

Similarly, biblical leaders must find a way to erect emotional boundaries when conflict occurs—boundaries that protect their hearts from overexposure and vulnerability—while at the same time maintaining the ability to lower those boundaries in order to give, serve, and love others freely. This inherently means that biblical leaders keep conflict "out there"—i.e., outside of themselves emotionally. They do so by not taking conflict personally, by viewing it objectively, and by cultivating an inner security that allows them to remain dispassionate when it occurs. This allows them the ability to listen to the opinions of others without being dependent upon those opinions; to walk through and learn from mistakes without condemning themselves as failures; to respect people without fearing them; to allow conflict to refine their rationale in decision-making without becoming fickle and indecisive; and to learn that they may love others while at the same time protecting their own hearts from dysfunctional people.

Jesus's security came from knowing who he was,
possessing integrity in what he did,
and from his depth of intimacy with the Father.

---

3. Learn from Conflict; Don't Always Leave It. With all that said, keeping conflict "out there" doesn't mean that the source of conflict is always someone else's fault. In truth, we often experience conflict in our lives and leadership because of our own actions, insecurities, and ill-motivated decisions. In these cases, conflict with others comes from within the self.

Since this is true, it is important for leaders to learn to ponder these kinds of hardships by first looking internally at what might be driving conflict with others—including their own lack of character and/or competence. Questions to consider include: Is this conflict caused by a poor decision, inadequate communication, or other lack of competence on my part? Am I acting as a servant-leader on behalf of others, or is this all about my ambitions, getting my way, and proving myself? Did this conflict result from my need for others' approval or fear of people? Did I enable this conflict to occur by allowing a dysfunctional culture to develop? Is the way we are structured for decisions systemically embedding conflict into our organization? The most honest and overriding question a leader can ask is, "What is the true and deepest source of this conflict?"

The first job of biblical leadership is to take responsibility. Even if a leader does not directly cause a problem, it is his or her job to fix it and to set structures in place to keep it from occurring again. Biblical leaders do not abdicate responsibility. Only when they own up to the portion they bring to challenges and conflict are they able to develop as the influencers God wants them to be (2 Timothy 2:21, Philippians 2:13, Hebrews 13:21) and change their organization for the better. You can learn great things from your mistakes when you aren't busy denying them.

When leaders recognize their missteps and confess them to the Lord, they place themselves in a context for divine sanctification. The process of true inner growth begins. Sanctification takes place when leaders admit before God and others their wrong—becoming more self-aware for the future; growing deeper in the character of Christ as steward, shepherd, and servant; and walking in God's grace daily. Unfortunately, what often happens instead is that leaders rob God of the ability to transform them because they ignore every conflict situation that comes up, fail to take responsibility, and never consider the possibility that God has brought a situation their way to use it for good. If we don't see conflict through the eyes of God and recognize it as something that has been sifted through his loving, sovereign hands, we will never grow from it. In truth, regardless of where fault lies in any given conflict, God is trying to speak to us in it— to reveal something to us about ourselves, to make us more dependent upon him, and to transform our character through the experience.

You can learn great things from your mistakes
when you aren't busy denying them.

When we ignore conflict by leaving situations where it occurs instead of facing up to it, *we take ourselves with us.* As Yogi Berra rightly said, "Wherever you go, there you are." In other words, though you have a new context, you still bring your self into it, and if you are the true cause of conflict, that conflict will show up again. Leaders change jobs, churches, roles, and even geographic locations, but they often do not change themselves. Amazingly, God has a loving way of bringing similar people and situations back into our lives to teach us the lessons we choose to ignore. More than any other priority he has for us as believers, it is his loving desire and purpose to develop within us the character of Christ (Romans 8:29). Character development is a prerequisite course in Christianity. If we choose to withdraw ourselves from class, God will automatically enroll us in a new one. The people may be different; the context may be different; but God will bring the same conflict our way—or better said, he will reveal once again the conflict that was within us the whole time. As Walt Kelly wrote it, "We have met the enemy, and he is us."[41]

Sadly, some leaders will spend years never learning the lessons found in conflict and end up repeating the same mistakes over and over, only with different people. The story is told of a man who, in the course of twenty years, held numerous jobs. He left each job due to similar problems. He claimed to have twenty years of experience, but in reality, he had *one experience repeated twenty times.* Why? Because he never learned the lessons he needed through these experiences.

Competency #5: Developing Those We Lead

Leaders have a choice in how they manifest their leadership. First, they can choose to *do*—that is, to do everything themselves. This strategy limits what can be achieved to the efforts and time of the leader. It also defies the heart of leadership—i.e., the ability to influence *others* to achieve a God-honoring objective. Second, leaders can *delegate*—that is, they can tell others to do tasks they would prefer not to do. Delegation is a popular notion in leadership today and is often discussed as a needed strategy for effectiveness. While delegation frees the leader to do other things, it does not reflect the noblest prospects of leadership. After all, one can tell a dog to fetch (i.e. delegate to it), but that's not really "leading" the dog—at least not as the Bible would describe leadership. Instead, the word that epitomizes what biblical leaders do in relationship to others is *develop*. Biblical leaders are called to develop those they lead, helping them to grow and reach their full potential in Christ and his kingdom. This goal connects to the loving character of the biblical leader and dignifies the follower by affirming that people are more than pawns for another's use. Developing those we lead goes to the heart of servant leadership—leading for the benefit of others. It also establishes a pattern for raising up something needed in every congregation: more people to lead. Ultimately, biblical leaders create more biblical leaders.

The heart of leadership is the ability to influence others
to achieve a God-honoring objective.

In Matthew 4, Jesus calls his first disciples, Peter and Andrew. Verse 19 says, "Follow me, and I will make you fishers of men." The word ποιέομαι, "will make," is a future active verb and may be rendered "will cause to be" or "will make to become."[42] Jesus is saying that he will do something toward these men that will cause them to "fish" for others (a play on words related to their original vocation and indicating that they would gather men into God's kingdom). Fast-forward three years, after the resurrection, to the end of Jesus's earthly ministry. In Matthew 28:19–20, Jesus says to his disciples, gathered on the mountain in Galilee, "Go therefore and make disciples of all nations, baptizing them in the name of the Father and of the Son and of the Holy Spirit, teaching them to observe all that I have commanded you. And behold, I am with you always, to the end of the age." At the beginning of Jesus's ministry, it was "I will make you." At the end of his ministry, it was "You go and make." These are the bookends to Jesus's time on the earth and in his interactions with the disciples.

The obvious question is: what did Jesus do in between? In other words, what did he do to take the disciples from the raw material of naïve novices to courageous champions of the gospel message? By looking closely across the Gospels and at Jesus's exchanges with the disciples, we witness three key ideas that achieve the goal of developing those we lead. They are *equip, empower* and *encourage.*

EQUIP	EMPOWER	ENCOURAGE
Mark 6:1–6 Jesus teaches in the synagogue	Mark 6:7–12 Jesus sends out the twelve	Mark 6:14–29 Death of John the Baptist
Mark 7:1–13 Jesus rebukes the Pharisees	Mark 6:30–43 Jesus feeds 5,000	Mark 6:45–52 Jesus walks on water
Mark 7:14–22 Jesus teaches the disciples about matters of the heart	Mark 8:1–10 Jesus feeds 4,000	Mark 7:24–37 Jesus heals a woman's daughter and a deaf man
Mark 8:11–20 Jesus teaches on unbelief		Mark 8:22–26 Jesus heals a blind man
Mark 8:31–37 Jesus foretells his death		Mark 8:27–30 Peter confesses Jesus

Mark 6–8 provide the best summary of Jesus's development of the disciples. In these chapters, Jesus employs the "equip, empower, and encourage" strategy. His development of the disciples through it is characterized in at least four ways:

1. *It was planned and spontaneous.* It seems in many instance that Jesus prepared and prearranged the kind of experiences that developed the disciples. But he didn't always cultivate them in a linear fashion. Rather, often his equipping, empowering, and encouraging occurred based upon the needs and opportunities of the moment. He used unarranged situations as powerful object lessons for their learning and growth.

2. *It was intentional.* It is obvious in these chapters that Jesus was purposefully preparing the disciples. He needed them to "get it," and he used both planned and impromptu ministry experiences with intention to achieve a particular overarching goal. Placing them in a context to experience ministry (by inviting them to follow him) he was able to provide them intentional development. With each encounter in this passage, we see a consistent thread of purpose. He was preparing them for the time when he would leave this earth, and he wanted them to understand that any need they faced would be met through faith in his supernatural power. This lesson would prove vital to their ministry after Jesus's resurrection and ascension.

3. *It was diverse.* Jesus wasn't monolithic in his development approach. As a master teacher, he used different learning techniques at different times and places in order to cultivate the disciples in potent and lasting ways. Sometimes the disciples were mere observers. Other times they were actual participants in the lesson. Jesus developed them on the hillside, on the sea, in a home, and at the temple. His mentoring took place in the morning, the daytime, and the evening.

4. *It was experiential.* Jesus's development of the disciples took place during the course of doing ministry. They were recruited and enrolled in a process, not simply sitting and listening. Jesus used the experiences contained within the adventure of ministry to grow them into maturity. It was true on-the-job development.

When we speak of equipping, empowering, and encouraging as necessary dynamics in the development of those we lead, we are talking about a focus of leaders toward their followers. Development of others means giving to those we lead what they need in order to reach their potential in Christ and in ministry. But what exactly does each component mean?

Equipping. This is the knowledge dimension of development. It includes directive behaviors from leaders to followers such as teaching, training, telling, and showing. The idea here is that those we lead must develop in their minds the knowledge necessary for the tasks given to them in order to know what to do and how to do it. Jesus equipped the disciples by teaching them and allowing them to hear him teach others (Mark 6:1–6, Mark 7:1–13, Mark 8:11–20, Mark 8:31–37). As well, they were able to learn how to handle different ministry situations by watching his interactions with all types of people. Today's leaders equip others by instructing and training them through individual "showing and telling" sessions, apprenticeships, on-the-job mentoring, or workshops, conferences, and seminars. The goal is for people to clearly know what to do and how to do it.

Empowering. This is the volitional dimension of development—that is, the engagement of the follower's will to the point of action. Here, the leader seeks to employ his or her followers in doing things that fulfill needs in the ministry but also lead to their individual growth. This goes beyond merely having them listen and watch. Empowering means involving followers in ministry with the goal of increasing their ownership and responsibility of it. Empowerment might include delegation, but this is not delegation merely for the purpose of relieving the leader of a task. It is delegation with the intent of increasing the confidence, efficacy, and self-actualization of the individual. It is to develop followers in such a way that they are made less dependent upon the leader, to the degree that eventually they are able to do the work themselves. Here, followers are inherently motivated because they connect their knowledge to their actual performance and prove themselves capable.

Jesus empowered the disciples by kicking them out their nest. He employed them to go and do ministry (Mark 6:1–1) and participate in the performance of his miracles (Mark 6:30–43, Mark 8:1–10). Indeed, people develop best by doing, but also by having ownership in what they do.

Leaders today empower others by giving them clear responsibility (written ministry/job descriptions, objectives, etc.), by permitting them to succeed or fail at such responsibilities, and by recognizing their achievements, ensuring that rewards for their work come back to them, not to the leader. This allows followers to connect the dots between their efforts and abilities and their actual effectiveness. When this happens, they begin to sense that they bring value to the organization and therefore strive further to fulfill their potential in work and ministry.

Encouraging. This is the emotional dimension of development. Theorists have concluded that individual change and development is much more lasting and successful when emotional and relational support are present.[43] Here, leaders do much more than impart knowledge and employ people in ministry. They lend supportive behaviors to those they lead— behaviors such as listening, praising, problem solving, asking for input, sharing rationale, and providing hopeful perspective when followers are discouraged. John 13–15 reveals Jesus's loving support to the disciples in preparation for his crucifixion and departure. He shares an intimate meal with them, washes their feet as a sign of his servant spirit toward them, and provides reassuring words about the future: "Let not your hearts be troubled" (John 14:1).

People are also encouraged and emboldened when they witness those they follow acting in consistent and competent ways. When leaders exemplify the message they preach (that is, they actually do what they are asking of their followers), and when the benefits and results actually come to pass as the leaders claimed they would, followers are inspired and heartened. They believe that they can "do it too" and see similar results. There is no doubt that when Jesus performed miracles before the eyes of the disciples, they were deeply encouraged both by the power of the message they were asked to believe and the credibility of the leader who was asking them to believe it (Mark 6:14–29, Mark 6:45–52, Mark 7:24–37, Mark 8:22–26, Mark 8:27–30). Such encouragement gave the disciples the emotional resources to move past any confusion or hardships they faced and begin to practice what they witnessed in their leader.

Leaders today can encourage those they lead by listening to them, sharing rationale about what is going on in the organization and why it's going on, giving them praise, showing them respect, asking about their family and personal needs, and providing encouragement when they lose heart. Additionally, when leaders live out before their followers the beliefs and behaviors consistent with their message, and when the positive results of such actions are evident, followers are reassured in what they are called to do and are emotionally encouraged to act in kind.

In conclusion, biblical leaders *equip the head, empower the hands*, and *encourage the heart* of those they lead. When they do, they help followers develop to their full potential in Christ and in ministry. People under them are fulfilled, become fruitful in ministry, and may become leaders themselves. This moves the practice of leadership to the highest possible good and reflects the heart of Christ in his leadership toward us. We go beyond being leaders who do, we go beyond being leaders of doers, and we become instead *leaders of leaders*. Doing so provides limitless opportunities for numeric growth within an organization, with a group being able to support more numbers because its growth is not limited by the efforts, gifts, and abilities of one person, and for qualitative health as the organization is infused with life and health as motivated people employ their gifts, grow in character and competence, and feel ownership of ministry. Additionally, leaders who equip, empower and encourage others find great personal fulfillment. They have the privilege of seeing others under them blossom and excel. Just like Jesus, these leaders leave a legacy of people who once needed change growing into change agents themselves.

Chapter Review Questions

1. List and briefly explain five principles of communication from Ephesians 4 and what leaders can do to apply them.
2. What are three ways a leader can becomes a great teacher? Explain each way.
3. Explain the bandwidth principle in communication.
4. 4. What does it mean to say "the issue is rarely the issue"?
5. What is culture according to Edgar Schein?
6. What does the leadership skill of creating culture mean? Explain.
7. Illustrate how Jesus understood and used the dynamics of culture.
8. What is the "snowball effect" of culture?
9. How can an organization possess diversity yet still enjoy a strong organizational culture?
10. How does culture correct and align people who are in it?
11. What is the only worthwhile reason for leading change? Explain.
12. What is the difference between our faith in the way God works and our faith in the God who works?
13. List the three phases of change, explain what each means, and illustrate each phase with the experience of Nehemiah.
14. What is the most important thing you have learned about leading change from the life of Nehemiah?
15. What is one reason conflict can be more prevalent and complicated in the church than outside of it?
16. What is the difference between tolerance and unity?
17. List the four steps of conflict resolution that Jesus outlined as recorded in Matthew
18. What are two of the benefits for those who follow this process as outlined by Jesus?
19. What is meant by the terms "scope of conflict" and "scale of conflict"? Explain the relationship between the two.

20. List the strategies for appropriate leader response to each category of conflict: (1) low scale/low scope; (2) low scale/high scope; (3) high scale/low scope; (4) high scale/high scope.
21. What does it mean to say, "Learn from conflict; don't always leave it"?
22. List and explain each of the three components of developing those we lead.

CHAPTER 6

COMMUNITY: THE PEOPLE OF THE LEADER

"When ministers and priests live their ministry mostly in their heads and relate to the Gospel as a set of valuable ideas to be announced, the body quickly takes revenge by screaming loudly for affection and intimacy. Christian leaders are called to live the Incarnation, that is, to live in the body, not only in their own bodies but also in the corporate body of the community, and to discover there the presence of the Holy Spirit."

HENRI J.M. NOUWEN

There can be no doubt that Jesus lived, died, and was resurrected with the goal of seeing people transformed. That is the primary way he brought glory to the Father. People—their redemption and transformation—were at the heart of Jesus's ministry, and despite all the challenges, frustrations, and distractions he faced, his leadership was intently directed toward these outcomes. As stated earlier in this book, biblical leadership is God-oriented and people-focused.

Yet, leadership in our day carries with it many potential diversions. Ironically, the subtlest and most detrimental is the drift away from leadership itself. That is to say, if we are not careful, we find ourselves doing many things as leaders—everything, in fact, except leading.

This drift is most characterized by a lack of focus upon people. As organizations continue to exist over time, bureaucratic and administrative demands become prevalent, and problems must be solved. "Putting out fires" captures the leader's time and attention. Program needs must be addressed and effective processes put in place—that is, the machine of the organization must run properly. These details are at the heart of good management. Yet often, the *important* tasks of influencing people in the organization are sacrificed for the *urgent* tasks of managing it. In time, leaders begin managing things more than leading people. This trend away from people and other leadership priorities is a costly mistake.

The subtlest and most detrimental
leadership distraction in our day
is the drift away from leadership itself.

Managing Things or Leading People?

While every entity must be managed well, and an organization's success will in fact be undermined without good management, management should not take place at the expense of leading. Rather, leaders must assign management its proper place and priority. Unfortunately, many organizations today are over-managed and under-led.

Organizations are over-managed for two primary reasons. First, many people mistakenly equate management with leadership. They haven't learned the core beliefs and behaviors of leadership that distinguish it from management—with the focus upon people being the highest of those distinctions. Second, it's actually easier to manage things than to lead people. Creating programs, maintaining processes, establishing policies—none of these things is nearly as challenging or messy as the stuff of leadership, which includes modeling character, directing people to fulfill calling, inspiring them with vision, building community, and developing people to their potential.

Management seeks to bring stability and predictability to an organization through administrative systems and regulations. Many people welcome such bureaucracy because it provides a sense of control and consistency and thus reduces anxiety. Leadership, on the other hand, challenges the status quo. It is disruptive in nature because it often provokes change. This may cause tension and ambiguity rather than stability and predictability. Management is mostly a present-tense orientation and asks, "What can be done now to ensure a well-functioning organization?" Leadership has a future orientation: it envisions an ideal future and moves people toward it. Management brings control through rules and regulations. Leadership seeks to give permission to and empower people rather than regulate them.

Unlike management, leadership is not concerned about the *efficiency* of an organization as much as its bottom-line *effectiveness*. Instead of asking, *"How* are we doing what we are doing?" (a concern for the way things are done), leadership inherently asks, *"Why* are we doing what we are doing?" (a concern for the purpose behind the actions). Leadership is focused upon people, with the outcome being their transformation. Management focuses on people too, but it does so from the standpoint of how they fit and function in the organization more than it addresses their fulfillment and fruitfulness. Leadership focuses people upon people. Management tends to focus people upon processes. Managers can view an organization as a functioning machine. Leaders view it as a living organism. In the words of both Peter Drucker and Warren Bennis: "Management is doing things right; leadership is doing the right things."[44]

Table: Concerns of Management vs. Leadership

MANAGEMENT	LEADERSHIP
Things (Programs, Processes, Policies)	People
Efficiency	Effectiveness
Maintenance	Mission
Control	Empowerment
Stability	Change
Human Resources	Human Transformation
Asks: How?	Asks: Why?

Despite the marked differences between them, management and leadership are not mutually exclusive. To be a good leader, one must manage some; and to be a good manager, one must be capable of leading to some degree.

When taken to their extremes, however, it is easy to see how management may rob a leader from actually leading—that is, management tends to defy leadership. Therefore, with all due respect to managers, leaders must be the ones who actually direct an organization and ultimately decide its priorities. If not, the proverbial tail will wag the proverbial dog. The *way* things are done becomes more important than the *why* of doing them. Leaders point people and resources toward what moves the organization forward to achieve mission, not necessarily toward what maintains it as it currently exists. Organizations without leadership experience a subtle spiral of slow death. Bureaucracies feed upon themselves, growing more encroaching and entrenched. Policies tend to over-police (notice the similarity in words), and there are never enough processes in place to satisfy those who must have control. Sadly, the energies and attention that should focus people toward growth and advancement are spent instead on matters of management. People's attention will be captured by something. It's the job of leaders to ensure it is captured by the right thing.

The slide away from leadership comes through a subtle deception: many of us think that activity is the same as productivity. It is not. Being busy is not necessarily being effective. Management keeps people busy, and bureaucracies create activity, but like the hamster on the wheel, it may all be going nowhere. The old preacher said, "If Satan can't make you bad, he makes you busy." Why is this true? Because Satan knows that both badness and busyness accomplish the same objective: futility. Biblical leaders stay crystal clear on the purpose for which they are leading. They align all their activities according to the outcomes they seek and resist any rivals that would deter them from the job of actually leading others.

Leadership focuses people upon people.
Management focuses people upon processes.

This battle between *doing things right* and *doing right things* was at the heart of Jesus's ministry—and most of the time, the choice between the two involved the core priority of people. The Pharisees repeatedly ridiculed Jesus's behavior because, while he did what was right, he often didn't do things the right way from their perspective. For example, rather than protect his religious reputation, Jesus was criticized for being close to "tax collectors and sinners" (Matthew 11:19). He was judged for healing on the Sabbath (doing right things) rather than ignoring a man in need due to religious rule keeping (doing things right) (Mark 3:1–6). Jesus, of course, knew that "the Sabbath was made for man, not man for the Sabbath" (Mark 2:27). Today we might say, "Management was made for leadership, not leadership for management." Additionally, instead of being obsessed with every minute oral law that reflected man-made traditions, Jesus focused upon the larger matter of reflecting God's heart (Mark 7:1–13). *Jesus broke almost every code of proper conduct in order to ensure that he did the right thing.* He held the law in proper perspective and thus kept the law in its proper place.

Looking closely at his choices, in most instances, we can see that doing the right thing revolved around the core subject of *people* and ministry toward them. The reason this discussion is so important is that from the Bible's perspective, as in the life of Jesus, leadership should be expressed in terms of impact upon and relationship to people. *People are the right thing.* This truth must be central in the biblical leader's mind; it must be the focus of his or her energies. As illustrated above, if we are not careful, we can easily lose our way as to the real goal of leadership. People are of immense value to God, more important than anything numeric, programmatic, managerial, or material, and our leadership should have the development and transformation of people as its object. *It is for people that Jesus died. It is for people that we lead.*

Therefore, building Christian community is at the heart of biblical leadership. The biblical leader knows that truly fulfilling and fruitful leadership flows from the virtue of love; that people thrive, benefit, and are best influenced within the power of Christian community; and that the outcome of biblical leadership is always about transforming the lives of human beings.

The Virtue of Love in Leadership

As their leader, Jesus loved his disciples. In fact, love was the primary motivating value in his leadership toward them. It was love that drove his desire to invest in them, to show grace and mercy toward them, to patiently develop them, and even to correct and rebuke them when they were in error. Jesus was deity and possessed all the power and privilege associated with that nature. Yet he contrasted the legalistic, distant, and harsh caricature of God common in his day with an unprecedented image of God that included love, care, and intimacy. As their God and leader, he told his disciples that he did not call them slaves but friends (John 15:15).

Likewise, biblical leaders love the people they lead. They are motivated by love for everyone they influence. In their closest relationships with followers, there is deep connection, vulnerability, understanding, and personal investment. Paul described his relationship to the Thessalonians just so: "Having so fond an affection for you, we were well-pleased to impart to you not only the gospel of God but also our own lives, because you had become very dear to us" (1 Thessalonians 2:8, NASB). Biblical leadership is grounded in the supreme moral virtue of agape love.

Love was the primary motivating value in Jesus's leadership.

Understanding Agape Love

Agape is the noun form of the Greek verb *agapao* and is "a love called out of one's heart by an awakened sense of value in the object loved that causes one to prize it."[45] The word is unique in the context of its day and is "practically a creation of the Christian church" as it "does not appear in classical Greek at all."[46]

Weust explains further:

> *Agapan* (Ἀγαπαν) never was a common word in classical literature, although it was in use from the beginning and occupied a distinctive place of its own. In Homer it is used only ten times, in Euripides but three. Its noun form *agapesis* (ἀγαπεσις) is rare. The form *agape* (ἀγαπε), so frequently found in the New Testament, does not occur at all. Its first appearance is in the Greek translation of the Old Testament. It conveyed the ideas of astonishment, wonder, admiration, and approbation when connected with the word *agamai* (ἀγαμαι) which meant, "to wonder at or admire." It was used in classical literature in the same sentence with *philein* (φιλειν) and had its distinctive sense of "a love of prizing" as contrasted to *philein* (φιλειν), "a love of liking." But owing to the very infrequency of its use, it was an admirable word which could be put to use to convey the new and higher conception of divine love which the New Testament presents. Its relative emptiness, so far as the general knowledge of the person was concerned who spoke Greek as his second language, made it the ideal receptacle into which the new moral and ethical content of Christianity could be poured . . . The pagan Greeks knew nothing of the love of self-sacrifice for one's enemy which was exhibited at Calvary. Therefore, they had no word for that kind of love. They knew nothing about the divine analysis of this love which Paul gives us in I Corinthians 13.[47]

In English, we may use the single word *love* to describe affection for a person ("I love my wife") and affection for an inanimate object ("I love my boat"). We inherently understand that though the same word is used, the meanings behind the word are different. In Greek, the primary language of the New Testament, there are four different words used to describe love. One portrays sexual love. Another means to express an interpersonal loving or liking based upon receiving pleasure or enjoyment. Still another describes familial love. Yet in the biblical texts, the term *agape* stands out as a unique manifestation of love. It is a noble word expressing the highest form of the concept. Weust states it eloquently:

> (Agapao) speaks of a love of esteem and approbation. The quality of this love is determined by the character of the one who loves, and that of the object loved.[48]

Agape is popularly thought of as selfless or altruistic love. In the New Testament, it often describes the kind of love God has for humans. Its emphasis is on the value placed upon the object loved—regardless of whether that object is inherently valuable, worthy, or deserving. Thus, the term also embraces the concept of unconditional love.

The uniqueness of agape across all definitions is that it flows from the character of the one giving it.[49] This is consistent with Scott Peck's view when he says that one of the major distinguishing features of love seems to be the "conscious or unconscious purpose in the mind of the lover."[50]

Love and Leadership

First-century Rome understood that man might die for God. *What they could hardly grasp was that God would die for man* (Romans 5:7–8). The idea that one in power and authority would give himself for the sake of others is a radical notion even in today's world. But it is exactly what the Bible teaches as it describes the idea of leadership. Look at these examples from the apostle Paul (the first is from his good-bye to the Ephesian elders in Acts; the others come from his letters):

> Therefore be alert, remembering that for three years I did not cease night or day to admonish every one with tears. And now I commend you to God and to the word of his grace, which is able to build you up and to give you the inheritance among all those who are sanctified. I coveted no one's silver or gold or apparel. You yourselves know that these hands ministered to my necessities and to those who were with me. In all things I have shown you that by working hard in this way we must help the weak and remember the words of the Lord Jesus, how he himself said, "It is more blessed to give than to receive." And when he had said these things, he knelt down and prayed with them all. And there was much weeping on the part of all; they embraced Paul and kissed him, being sorrowful most of all because of the word he had spoken, that they would not see his face again. And they accompanied him to the ship. (Acts 20:31–38)

> I thank my God in all my remembrance of you, always in every prayer of mine for you all making my prayer with joy, because of your partnership in the gospel from the first day until now. And I am sure of this, that he who began a good work in you will bring it to completion at the day of Jesus Christ. It is right for me to feel this way about you all, because I hold you in my heart, for you are all partakers with me of grace, both in my imprisonment and in the defense and confirmation of the gospel. For God is my witness, how I yearn for you all with the affection of Christ Jesus. And it is my prayer that your love may abound more and more, with knowledge and all discernment, so that you may approve what is excellent, and so be pure and blameless for the day of Christ, filled with the fruit of righteousness that comes through Jesus Christ, to the glory and praise of God. (Philippians 1:3–11)

Therefore, my brothers, whom I love and long for, my joy and crown, stand firm thus in the Lord, my beloved. (Philippians 4:1)

But since we were torn away from you, brothers, for a short time, in person not in heart, we endeavored the more eagerly and with great desire to see you face to face, because we wanted to come to you—I, Paul, again and again—but Satan hindered us. (1 Thessalonians 2:17–18)

Jesus commanded and commissioned agape in his disciples. He said, "A new commandment I give to you, that you love one another: just as I have loved you, you also are to love one another" (John 13:34). Our love, unity, and mutual support was such a priority for Jesus that one of his last prayers on the earth contained the plea, "Holy Father, keep them in your name, which you have given me, that they may be one, even as we are one" (John 17:11b). In Jesus's mind, agape was to be the distinguishing mark that identified us as his true followers: "By this all people will know that you are my disciples, if you have love for one another" (John 13:35). Love, unity, and community are at the heart of following Jesus, and they therefore must be central to both the practice of leadership and the product that leadership gains.

First-century Rome understood that man might die for God. What they could hardly grasp was that God would die for man.

Agape serves as the catalyst for a type of leadership that benefits others and evokes a response within them to follow and trust the leader. The foremost purpose in the mind of a servant leader is to place authentic value upon people, to affirm their worth and prize them, and to do so in such a way that he or she influences them in a manner best for them. Agape-based leadership moves past leadership for the benefit of self and toward leadership for the benefit of others. And since any discussion about leadership is a discussion about the ability to influence people, we must understand that agape holds the greatest power to do exactly that. *Love changes people unlike any other force.* It also ensures that a leader's influence is moral. Agape provides a moral motivation for influence and an impetus for moral choices in the means by which one influences— and at the end of that influence, it almost assuredly produces a moral outcome. Nothing embodies godliness such as loving influence like this.

The worth of such a virtue may be catching on beyond the Bible. There is strong external evidence to suggest love's value in leadership, management, and organizational effectiveness. Mitroff and Denton, in their ninety interviews with high-level managers and executives, found that "terms such as love, respect, trust, and wisdom are used freely and the concepts they represent are readily accepted."[51] Waitely, speaking of success in a knowledge-based world, sees love as the subject that underlies all themes in leadership: "Leaders respond to the needs of others. Most leaders used to demand respect for themselves; the new leader cares much more about creating opportunities for people to respect themselves."[52] In Kouzes and Posner's seminal work on leadership, they claim that good leaders show compassion to followers.[53] DePree includes love among the attributes of effective leaders.[54] Steven Covey, in his groundbreaking book on leader effectiveness, speaks of the need for unconditional love within the hearts of all who seek to influence:

> In other words, when we truly love others without condition, without strings, we help them feel secure, safe, validated, and affirmed in their essential worth, identity, and integrity. Their natural growth process is encouraged. We make it easier for them to live the laws of life—cooperation, contribution, self-discipline, integrity—and to discover and live true to the highest and best within them.[55]

In Jesus's mind, agape was to be the distinguishing mark of his true followers.

Finally, James A. Autry in his book *Love and Profit: The Art of Caring Leadership* provides real-life stories of the power of love at work in organizations. In one example, he speaks of a leader at a Fortune 500 company who chooses love toward his employees by meeting their needs at special, critical moments in life:

> A few years ago a very bright and productive salesperson in my group came to me with a special request. Her husband was being transferred about a hundred miles away from the city in which our offices were located. Because of child-care problems in the new location, she wanted to be allowed to remain on full-time employment but work at home two days a week, coming to the office only three days a week. She promised to keep up her accounts and remain as effective as ever.
>
> I agreed to give it a try. There was resentment, most of which, surprisingly, came from other women on the staff. The personnel director didn't like it at all. "Bad precedent and outside policy." And my boss didn't like it very much, either, for the same reasons.
>
> At this point you think I'm about to glory in my vindication. Not true. It did not work out. But it did not stop me from trying another outside-the-policy accommodation for a new mother who convinced her managers and me that she could do productive, high-quality work by mixing office and home time. She simply wanted to be with her first child at home, longer than policy allowed. Her record was good. Her commitment to her work and to the company effort was unyielding, and her work itself was of outstanding quality. And in this case the special treatment worked perfectly: for the company, for her, and, I trust, for the baby.
>
> I've made exceptions to corporate rules to help get an employee's family through the nightmare of overwhelming financial and emotional distress. I've made similar exceptions for employees needing assistance to recover from substance abuse . . . In every office you hear the threads of love and joy and fear and guilt, the cries for celebration and reassurance, and

somehow you know that connecting those threads is what you are supposed to do and business will take care of itself.[56]

The above not only illustrates a leader who chooses to do the right thing as opposed to simply and always doing things right, it also gives evidence that there are many leaders who value love in the heart of leadership who also possess the conviction that it is not mutually exclusive to profits. They explode the myth that "nice guys finish last," and in fact, they would advocate that creative, caring leadership—i.e. agape love—has the power to produce many benefits for organizations when exercised properly. They would also say that love in leadership is personally gratifying, as it becomes an extension of the leader's self, allowing him or her to consistently exist in the world for its betterment. It allows the leader to sleep a little easier at night by questioning the assumption that one must sacrifice integrity and peace of mind in favor of organizational success.

Influence in Community

Biblical leadership always exists to accomplish a God-glorifying purpose, and the accomplishment of this purpose involves leaders and followers working in relationship with each other. Jesus didn't simply tell the disciples to show up at the temple once a week, and there he would lecture them. Jesus did life with those he led. As together they served in itinerant ministry (Matthew 9:35–39, Mark 2:15, Mark 9:30, Luke 10:38), there were powerful, celebratory moments (Matthew 7:28–29, Matthew 14:13–21, Matthew 28:1–10, Luke 17:11–19, John 11:38–44), confusing and confounding times (Matthew 16:23, Mark 8:14–21, Mark 14:50, John 13:21–30), and plenty of normal, everyday interactions. They shared joys and hardships alike. Jesus chose to impart *himself*, not just his teaching. It was in the context of this community between him and his disciples, experiencing failures and victories alike, that they achieved something of great value together. Thus, the quality of relationships between leaders and those they lead will often determine the level of success they achieve. *People are best influenced and yield greater achievements within Christian community.*

As Jesus and his disciples served in itinerant ministry,
there were powerful, celebratory moments; confusing and
confounding times; and plenty of normal, everyday interactions.

Characteristics of Christian Community

Since biblical leadership succeeds best within the context of Christian community, strong, unified relationships provide the soil where the seed of leadership flourishes. The opposite is true as well. When there is disunity and dissatisfaction, leadership flounders. That's why it's important for leaders to concern themselves not only with the mission they seek to achieve through others, but also with the relationships between those who are involved in achieving that mission. Good leaders manage both the task at hand and the quality of the relationships people possess who are doing the task.

In Acts 2:42–47, the Scripture provides a beautiful and compelling picture of Christian community. This snapshot of the early church offers a template for Christian community that all biblical leaders should seek to follow. If leaders would build these traits into the relationships among those they lead, not only would they inspire passion within people to achieve mission, but also God would honor and bless such community.

1. Full Devotion to Christ and His Cause

They devoted themselves to the apostles' teaching and to fellowship, to the breaking of bread and to prayer. (v. 42)

Leaders must be used to model and teach the truth that halfhearted, semidevoted people rarely accomplish anything of value. Part of the character of a God-honoring community is full devotion and passion toward the things that matter most. People are uninspired by leaders who set before them unworthy causes or expect anything less than their very best to achieve mission.

2. Anticipation of God's Supernatural Work

> Everyone was filled with awe at the many wonders and signs performed by the apostles. (v. 43)

People want to be a part of something God-sized. In truth, God stands ready to work in and through a willing community. Here in Acts 2, people prayed and expected God to answer. We should build teams and organizations that think about and pray to achieve that which can only be accomplished through God's supernatural power.

3. A Strong Commitment to One Another

> All the believers were together and had everything in common. (v. 44)

Leaders replicate within their people the values they themselves possess. This occurs at a rather subconscious level. The stories leaders tell, the energies they expend, the behaviors they model—all these communicate to others what is important in the mind and heart of the leader, and by default, what's not important. Leaders must authentically value people and relationships, not only tasks and outcomes. They must likewise teach those they lead the priority of people and the virtues that express that priority, including such things as loyalty, dependability, mutual support, respect, and grace to others.

4. Generosity in Meeting Needs

> They sold property and possessions to give to anyone who had need. (v. 45)

In the course of work and achieving mission, needs arise within individuals. People become disheartened. They experience distress. They incur personal hardships that on the surface may have little connection to the work they are doing. Biblical leaders understand that people, whether consciously or not, bring their personal matters with them into every area of their lives. Therefore, in biblical community, people are not blind to the needs of others, and they respond by seeking to assist, encourage, and generously meet needs. In highly effective groups, sincere care and concern takes place between group members.

5. Laughter and Fellowship

> Every day they continued to meet together in the temple courts. They broke bread in their homes and ate together with glad and sincere hearts. (v. 46)

People in healthy Christian community enjoy downtime. They know they must give effort and hard work, but they also spend a measure of time in fellowship and relaxation. They eat together, laugh together, and pursue common interests outside of work or "ministry." This provides levity to offset the sometimes-difficult labor that people are doing, and it also allows them to get to know each other in a context beyond the work environment. This reaps the benefit of even greater unity and commitment.

6. A Sense of Shared Destiny from God

> . . . praising God and enjoying the favor of all the people. And the Lord added to their number daily those who were being saved. (v. 47)

Along with the sense of awe that resulted from seeing God answer prayer, those in the first church saw evidence that God was doing something outside their requests or expectations. They saw that God was doing a work of his own and that they were connected to a power beyond them. This was a work that transcended their efforts and connected them to God's eternal purpose. God was transforming the real lives of people through divine salvation and was bringing them into this church. I imagine that as they witnessed life after life, person after person coming to faith, this created a sense of shared destiny—a feeling that they were being swept along by the current of God's Holy Spirit for some sovereign purpose and were joined by God himself to his eternal plan.

This final trait of community is one that cannot be manufactured by a leader or his or her people. It is in fact a divine result of community—in other words, a gift of grace. But be sure that, while people cannot produce this sense of shared destiny, they can certainly undermine it or even prevent it from arising. They do this by failing to seek to build the kind of authentic community God desires between his children. Christian community is the receptacle for God's sovereign and supernatural work.

Community and the Leader

Sadly, leadership today is often associated with loneliness. Leaders forget that they are human too—that they too need community. They believe that unlike other people in the world, they can operate in superhuman ways, where week after week their needs for acceptance, companionship, and appreciation go unmet.

While leaders and followers must observe appropriate levels of intimacy and discretion, biblical leaders should not feel isolated from those they lead. In fact, in Jesus's ministry we see the exact opposite. He was intimately involved in relationship with a small group of men, and in a human sense, he was dependent upon the power he received from those relationships (John 13–15).

Christian community is the receptacle
for God's sovereign and supernatural work.

Jesus established appropriate levels of intimacy and openness in the relationships he enjoyed. Some were in relationship with Jesus on a superficial level. Many of the large crowd who followed him fell into this category. Others were allowed by Jesus to relate more deeply in community with him (for example, Peter, James, and John). Jesus was more vulnerable, trusting, and open with those in the closest circle than with others. These levels allowed for appropriate boundaries and protection, yet also provided Jesus (as fully human) the ability to be fed and fueled by friendship and love.

For leaders today, what is shared and given to those on the outer level of relationship should look different from the openness and vulnerability toward those closest to them.

What does this look like in a practical sense? At the congregational or larger organizational level, leaders may share personal stories, joys, and hardships, yet do so without giving intimate detail. For example, an authentic leader can admit that he is still learning to love his spouse without sharing details of the argument they had last week. There is a need for some openness even with those in the larger organization. This allows a leader not to feel like a fake before his or her people, and it also allows all members of the organization to sense that he or she is a real person just like them. This approach, when handled properly, lends credibility to the leader.

Authenticity at every level is the goal. However, authenticity does not mean sharing every dark detail with everyone and wearing every emotion on one's sleeve. *Authenticity means not misrepresenting oneself to others*—i.e., not deceiving people so they think the leader is something he or she is not. Leaders can be authentic without being overexposed or inappropriately vulnerable with people.

The level of openness between leaders and those they lead increases as relationships move closer to the leader—provided of course, that there is safety in those people and relationships. Safe relationships are the key. Leaders must somehow find connections where they are safe to commune in ways that shine light in the dark places of their hearts, allowing them to admit their hurt or pain and confess their mistakes or sins or what they might feel shame about, and also celebrate with others when successes occur.

Levels of Community:

This deepest kind of love and intimacy is essential for leaders as human beings, yet it should only be shared with a few, and discretion is necessary. As the proverb says, "A man of *too many* friends comes to ruin, but there is a friend who sticks closer than a brother" (Proverbs 18:24, emphasis mine). Let's face it—not all people are safe. Many of us have felt the pain of betrayal and rejection from those we thought loyal and trustworthy. This reality threatens particular harm to leaders, who may lose followers or reputation because of a person who uses intimate information for harmful purposes.

Some leaders who have been burned recoil to the point of isolation. They determine that it's better to be isolated than risk being wounded. In their minds, the risk of vulnerability and overexposure is just too great. But the risks simply do not undo the fact that deep relationships are critical for every leader. They give relational life, emotional health, and long-term staying power. How many leaders do you know who could have salvaged their marriages, families, or leadership positions if only they'd had true openness and intimacy in relationship with someone else? What if they could have confessed to a safe friend a financial struggle, a flirtatious temptation, an addictive behavior, a deep hurt, or their personal weariness in leadership? How many of them could have been saved from internal collapse?

Leaders must practice what the apostle James stated: "Therefore, confess your sins to one another, and pray for one another so that you may be healed. The effective prayer of a righteous man can accomplish much" (James 5:16).

Leaders must find connections where they are safe
to shine light in the dark places of their hearts.

Building Community

Leaders tend to think that the task at hand is the most important thing in the minds of those they lead—starting a new church, developing a ministry program, planning to construct a building, etc. They believe that people feel the same measure of motivation about the achievement of a particular mission as they do. In reality, *mission might get people to join you, but relationships are what keep people from leaving you.* Leaders must get this. Those we lead desire community! Community is the staying power of serving in ministry, more so than the achievement of an important goal or task. People feel inspired as a result of working with others. This is why the causes we seek to achieve should be pursued in the context of Christian community. Otherwise, we are not reflecting God's intention in the achievement of the things to which he calls us: namely, to build people in the process of achieving tasks. We also risk the possibility of losing people in the long term. In Christ, as we achieve something together we also *become* something together (Acts 2:42-47). We become a God-honoring community, used by him to accomplish something of great value!

God seeks to do something between people as he does something through them. When people who minister together feel a common connection and share their lives with one another in the course of achievement, they stay inspired. Said another way, it might be for a cause that people start a task. It is for community that people endure in that task and feel great reward at the end of it.

Since biblical leadership takes place in the context of Christian community, how does a leader actually build the kind of unifying relationships that achieve God-honoring goals? What are the practices and dynamics at play?

God seeks to do something between people
as he does something through them.

The Asset of Trust

At the foundation of every relationship is the dynamic of trust. Without it, you don't have relationship. Trust is the invisible currency of relationship: it is at the heart of what is exchanged between people. We give trust to others and receive it from others. We trust people to accept us, listen to us, value us, support us, and act in ways that are best for us. We also provide the same to others. Consequently, the level of trust among people determines the degree of connection and community they will feel. The greater the trust, the deeper the love and unity.

As a leader, if people trust you, they will follow you. If they don't trust you, they won't follow you—at least not in the long term. Thus, it could be said that trust is the primary asset of biblical leadership. It is what leaders must create in order to gain inherent permission from others to inspire and influence them in the most Christlike way.

Back in chapter 2, the Social Theory of leadership was introduced. This is the idea that leadership comes from mutually beneficial social exchanges between leaders and followers. Expanding on this, theorists have portrayed all leadership as built upon a dyad (defined as that which consists of two elements), or to use the more technical phrase, *vertical dyadic linkage*.[57] Simply put, this means that the effectiveness of leadership correlates to the quality of the dyadic relationship between leader and follower. It also explains that each leader, whether he or she actually knows an individual follower or not, has a relationship with that follower because the follower perceives that relationship to exist. Regardless of how many people work in an organization or the degree to which a leader actually knows the individuals within it, these individuals hold some form of trust and relationship with the leader. This is why the public perception of the CEO of a large corporation is so vitally important, or the way that a pastor of a large church is perceived. Whether these leaders know everyone in the organization or not, everyone feels that they know them. Consequently, not only do leaders need to build trust with people they actually know and invest in (those at the core of the organization), they must also act in ways that build trust across the organization. This is their *trust persona*, if you will, and it is vitally important. Hopefully, it is also authentic to who they truly are.

Not only do leaders need to build trust
with people they actually know,
they must also act in ways that build trust across the organization.

Think of it this way. A leader holds a joint "account" with every person in the organization. We might call it the trust account. Just like a bank account, leaders make deposits into and/or withdrawals from the trust account on an ongoing basis. Deposits include such things as acting competently, showing integrity, giving care and concern, offering self-sacrifice, and providing good communication. Withdrawals might include initiating change, expecting sacrifice and extra work, leading bold initiatives into uncharted waters, correcting errant behavior, or asking people to endure through difficult times rather than give up. Many leaders make more withdrawals than deposits into the trust account. Consequently, when the time comes that a leader needs his or her people to trust and follow despite a lack of rationale and resources, followers don't. As with a bank account, more withdrawals than deposits equal insufficient funds. The trust check bounces.

Smart leaders make ongoing deposits of trust. They do this primarily because it's the right thing to do under God. But they also understand that there is an important side benefit. When push comes to shove, leaders who have built trust (i.e., they have acted trustworthily) are those who will be trusted. People will say, "I might not see it this way or agree with the leader, but I trust this person and I will follow them."

Biblical leaders understand that trust is earned not simply given. Leaders build trust in four primary ways:

1. Character- A Trust of Consistency: When leaders act in integrity, they are believable and thus trusted. They keep agreements, behave consistently, act fairly and sacrifice for the sake of others and the organization. They display moral character.
2. Care & Concern- A Trust of Regard for Others: when followers perceive that leaders care for them, listen to them, have concern for them, and genuinely hold their best interests in mind, they trust these leaders.
3. Competence- A Trust of Capability: Leaders who make good decisions and exercise skillfulness are leaders who build credibility.

They are seen as dependable because they possess competencies in what they are doing, and those competencies help the organization succeed. Leaders who hold a track record of success enable followers to have confidence in them for the future. Their history of competence builds trust. A history of incompetence makes trust difficult for followers.

4. Communication- A Trust of Authenticity: Sharing information about the organization, sharing information about oneself, telling the truth, admitting mistakes, giving constructive feedback, maintaining confidentiality—these build reciprocal trust, because by communicating to followers, a leader is trusting them. (See chapter 4 and the "Skill of Communication" for more detail on communication.)

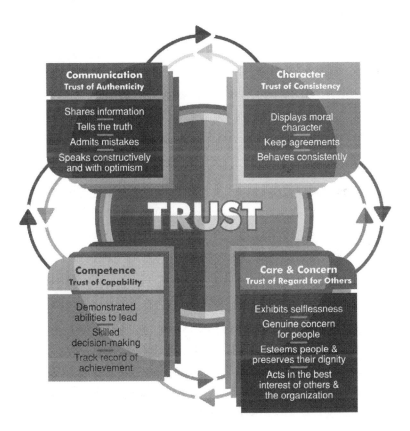

Practical Community Building

With a foundation of trust laid, community can be built. Several practical actions and principles help leaders build the kind of authentic community that makes leadership personally fulfilling and blesses those with whom they work.

1. *Build community one relationship at a time.* There really are no shortcuts for building community. It takes time to sit with people, get to know them, and prove that you genuinely care. Sending out an e-mail or having a group meeting helps you communicate information, but it's no substitute for getting to know a real person.

2. *Make time for downtime.* Setting aside planned time to "build relationships" can make it seem forced or programmed. *Build relationship all the time in brief, everyday interactions with people.* Take a minute to ask someone how he or she is doing. Say hello to people you pass in the hallway. This may seem basic, but a friendly word or smile can make someone's day. In other words, *be friendly and make a connection.*

3. *Listen more than you talk.* Leaders are famous for loving to hear themselves talk— and to mostly talk about themselves. Seek to listen to others more than you speak (James 1:19). If you ask people about their life and world, and take the time to listen attentively, they will become drawn to you and more readily trust you. This means sincere care, not pretend listening.

4. *Try to remember names.* You will be amazed at the response if you remember someone's name after meeting him or her the first time. This one practice attracts people toward a leader like almost nothing else. It shows your interest in the other person and dignifies their presence with you.

5. *Go where people are.* If you want to build community, you have to go to the places where other people go: picnics, parks, events, parties, playgrounds, youth soccer games, etc. Don't isolate yourself from people. They matter.

6. *Accept people as they are.* Some leaders communicate in sub-conscious ways that others just don't measure up. Leaders who constantly critique and come across as judgmental are leaders no one wants to be around.

7. *Work with people; don't use them.* It's inauthentic to form relationships just to get people to do things for you. That approach won't work in the long term because people will feel used. Leaders should approach relationships with integrity. We form relationships because we genuinely care and because we share a common mission. Of course, we cannot be friends with everyone. Determine the appropriate level of a relationship, establish boundaries with it, and act authentically within those boundaries. *Remember, however: the more you ask of someone, the more need there is to have relationship with him or her.* Making demands of people without a measure of care, concern, and trust for them creates resentment.

8. *Be relational; don't just act relational.* People quickly learn whether you genuinely enjoy people or are bothered by them. Again, appropriate boundaries are needed because there are many demands upon a leader's time, but how you are perceived *is* important—and perception flows from what is actually in the heart of the leader. Ask God to give you a genuine love for people. If you genuinely enjoy people, whether you can spend a lot of time with them or not, others will be attracted by your attitude.

9. *A note about time.* It's not logical to assume that leaders can spend quality time with every person in the organization. However, biblical leaders determine the key people with whom they will have quality relationships, and they go about investing in them by the example of Jesus. This number can normally be no greater than ten to twelve (notice that Jesus engaged twelve disciples). Beyond this number, time is a constraint and relationships enter into a different category of intensity and intimacy. In other words, *you cannot build community with all, but you must have it with a*

few. Normally, many of these key people will be those with whom the leader interacts on mission and on a regular basis. While leaders should be genuine with everyone, it is wise to invest at this level with people who hold pivotal roles in an organization. This matter of ten to twelve not only aligns with the time bandwidth of leaders, but also with the emotional bandwidth. We only have a maximum amount of time to be able to invest in this number of relationships, but we also possess a maximum emotional capacity that tops off at about the same number. Most of us don't possess the emotional resources to genuinely care, be concerned for, and build authentic relationship with more than that. Understanding these limitations actually helps leaders be more effective toward the ones God has given them.

10. *Building friendships.* Finally, leaders should give themselves permission to have the deepest of friendships and it is healthy for these relationships to exist outside the church or organization. These kinds of friendships provide downtime and companionship, wise counsel outside the loop of the organization, healthy accountability, and loving support during difficult seasons. A good pattern for healthy leadership seems to be one or two safe, deep friendships with people of the same gender and who stand outside the leader's core group, church or organization.

People Are the Big Deal

I once heard about a pastor who loved crowds, but didn't like people all that much. Sadly, this can be said of many leaders. They want people around because they need people to do things for them. Yet they don't really care for them. Such leaders do not consider their own effectiveness in terms of how to serve and better the lives of those people. A biblical leader is an individual called of God to interact with and impact people. Biblical leadership is not primarily about developing a ministry program, sitting behind a computer, creating a policy, or constructing a building. It is not about profits, widgets, or organization size. These may be a means toward a people-transforming end, but they are never the ends in themselves. Instead, *people are the primary outcome of biblical leadership—people who are influenced, impacted, and transformed.*

The Sermon on the Mount in Matthew 5–7 contains the most profound teaching the world has ever known. Jesus's words were radical, relevant, and revealing. He introduced startling and life-changing concepts about God, life in God's kingdom, and the way relationships should work between humans. His message on the hillside that day has earned the reputation of being the greatest sermon in history. Matthew records that when Jesus concluded, people were absolutely amazed at his teaching (Matthew 7:28–29). In fact, they were so amazed that Jesus immediately became a celebrity: "When Jesus came down from the mountain, large crowds followed Him" (Matthew 8:1). Jesus could have taken the show on the road, greatly increased the number of people following him, and fueled his popularity even further. Some people live for such an opportunity for glory! I imagine his disciples were thinking the sky was the limit as to Jesus's popularity and to the power they could gain because of it.

Instead of growing the crowds after the Sermon on the Mount, Jesus moved into ministry toward individuals.

Jesus, however, did something dramatically different than most people expected. Rather than continue to build his popularity and increase the size of his crowd, the Bible tells us that after that shining moment, Jesus withdrew. He avoided the multitudes and sought to fade from the public eye (Matthew 8:18). *Instead of growing his popularity, he moved into ministry toward individuals.* He lovingly touched a leper and healed him (Matthew 8:1–4). He restored a centurion's servant (Matthew 8:5–13, Luke 7:1–10). He witnessed a funeral taking place and spotted a woman in the procession who was not only already a widow, but also who was now burying her only son (Luke 7:11–15). Luke says that when he saw her, "He felt compassion for her" (Luke 7:13). The Greek word used here is *splanchnidzomai*, and it is a strong word denoting a visceral, gut-level reaction.[58] This was not some fleeting emotion Jesus felt. It could be translated, "His heart went out to her."

It's quite amazing that after Jesus's big moment he would notice individual people and their needs. One would think his growing fame and popularity would be the big deal for him. It certainly was for many others. *But for Jesus, individual people didn't detract from the big deal. They were the big deal.* Even with multitudes around him, he had the vision to see others not merely as crowds or groups, but as individuals to be loved. It was out of this vision that he sought to pour himself into them for their sake. Though crowds were changed and multitudes followed, Jesus's vision was life-by-life, person-by-person.

Just as with Jesus, we must remember that biblical leadership is about people. In the Scripture, every time God called a leader to a leadership task, his purpose was to redeem and restore his people through the instrument of the leader. Leaders who don't evaluate their leadership in these terms, who don't enjoy people, or who do not focus themselves on being used for others' sake are leaders who will not reflect the heart of God in their leadership. Leaders who celebrate people, tell stories of life change, and are moved by God's work in others are leaders who "get it" when it comes to the heart of God.

Jesus had the vision to see others
not merely as crowds or groups,
but as individuals to be loved.

All this points to one final, important concept. Not only is it foremost in a biblical leader's mind to see people's lives changed by the power of God, it is a leader's primary joy. Nothing gratifies the biblical leader like relationships with people, the satisfaction of seeing people give themselves fully to Christ and his cause, and watching others blossom through the use of their gifts and abilities in the kingdom.

One picture in the New Testament captures better than any other the power and beauty of relationship that is possible between a leader and his or her followers. In Acts 20, the Apostle Paul says goodbye to the Ephesian elders. After spending three years at this church, the time has come for him to board ship and leave. He reminds them of his boldness in declaring the gospel "with tears and with trials" (vss. 18-21) and announces that he is going to Jerusalem "not knowing what will happen to me there, except that the Holy Spirit testifies to me in every city that imprisonment and afflictions await me." (vss. 22-23) Paul tells them it is unlikely that they will see his face again, warns them of coming false teachers, and in his final words commends them "to God and to the word of his grace" (vs. 32).

Then the writer Luke describes a beautiful scene there at the harbor near Ephesus where Paul and the people he led and loved, and who in return deeply loved him, embraced, wept and knelt together in prayer.

> And when he had said these things, he knelt down and prayed with them all. And there was much weeping on the part of all; they embraced Paul and kissed him, being sorrowful most of all because of the word he had spoken, that they would not see his face again. And they accompanied him to the ship. (Acts 20:36-38)

What a majestic picture! It is the picture of the potential for people who work together on mission (leaders and followers alike) to become something together in the process. And in the end, beyond all the good things that are achieved, the most gratifying aspects of the biblical leader's work are the people with whom he loved and led.

Paul certainly understood this. For him as well as for Jesus, they were the big deal and his great joy and crowing achievement was ministry to them and with them.

"For what is our hope or joy or crown of boasting before our Lord Jesus at his coming? Is it not you? For you are our glory and joy." (1 Thessalonians 2:19–20).

Chapter Review Questions

1. Explain how leaders drift to managing things instead of leading people.
2. Why are many organizations over-managed and under-led?
3. Describe five differences between management and leadership.
4. Is being busy the same as being effective? Explain.
5. Give one example of when Jesus chose to do the right thing as opposed to doing things the right way.
6. Explain three ways that Christian community is at the heart of biblical leadership.
7. Explain one characteristic of agape love and its relevance to leadership.
8. Is love in leadership exclusive of profits? Explain how love could actually benefit the bottom line of a for-profit organization.
9. List six characteristics of Christian community from Acts 2 that all leaders should aspire to attain in their groups or organizations.
10. Explain authenticity in leadership and its relationship to the different levels of community.
11. Fully explain the concept of the "trust account" in leadership.
12. What are three primary ways leaders build trust?
13. What does it mean to say that people are the primary outcome of biblical leadership?
14. Give a biblical example of how individual people were the big deal for Jesus.
15. What traits in Paul's leadership allowed him to grow to love those he led, and for them to love him?

CHAPTER 7

CHRIST: THE POWER OF THE LEADER

"It is not great men who change the world, but weak men in the hands of a great God."

Brother Yun

A recent search of Amazon.com, the world's largest book retailer, revealed over two hundred thousand books currently in print that deal specifically with the subject of leadership. A Google search of the keyword *leadership* returned over one million web pages and online articles. Each year countless workshops, forums, and training seminars in business, church, and nonprofit organizations are held to equip people to be better leaders. Over recent decades, the academic community has offered a multitude of scientific theories regarding the phenomenon of leadership. Leadership centers, educational degrees and certifications, and leadership coaches and consultants are in vogue.

Never has there been more information, literature, and training about the subject of leadership. Yet, the nation's moral decay and the lack of church influence in our culture suggests that leadership has never been more poorly practiced. In truth, leaders don't need more knowledge. *They need more power to lead like Christ.*

True power to lead comes from something greater than learning about leadership. It is first about experiencing power. Potent and transformative influence after the pattern of Christ is beyond the intellect and strength of any individual. To lead as a servant, steward, and shepherd; to influence others from a sense of deep calling and purpose; to express competencies that are divinely empowered; and to eternally impact the lives of people that matter to God, we must tap into a supernatural source. Christ himself is the power by which the biblical leader lives, loves, and leads.

A Relationship of Power

As a matter of historical record, two thousand years ago a group of rabbinical disciples were devastated when their leader, Jesus, was crucified. At his death they were confused, scattered, and afraid. And then something happened. Sunday happened. The resurrection happened! Whether one is a follower of Jesus or not, all must admit that something historically occurred that changed everything with this group. They were completely convinced that the same power that raised Jesus from the grave was now available to them for real human living. This conviction changed them—and it literally changed the world.

The revolution that came on the heels of Jesus's resurrection was primarily effected from within. Christianity was not (and is not) about external conformity to a set of standards. When Jesus was resurrected and ascended into heaven, he did not leave behind a religion to practice. He did not leave merely a moral code, a list of rules and regulations, or a set of values by which to live. Instead, he imparted the very person of the Holy Spirit to indwell believers. His idea was to empower his followers from that day forward through *a living relationship with a loving God.* This relationship is intended to be personal, intimate, and transforming. The resurrection means life—certainly life for Jesus, but also life available for us. In Christ, there is the promise of power!

> May the God of peace, who through the blood of the eternal covenant brought back from the dead our Lord Jesus, that great Shepherd of the sheep, equip you with everything good for doing his will, and may he work in us what is pleasing to him, through Jesus Christ, to whom be glory for ever and ever. Amen. (Hebrews 13:20–21)
>
> . . . for it is God who works in you, both to will and to work for his good pleasure. (Philippians 2:13)

The glory of Christian living is that God calls us to do his will and then gives us the ability to do it. God calls us to holiness and then empowers that holiness within. God calls us to serve, to lead, and to obey and then enables these responses in us by his own strength and presence. In other words, when God gives his will, he also imparts the power by which to achieve it. This reality makes Christianity more than a religion, an ethic, or an idle dream. God himself becomes the very energy for every expectation he sets: "Christ in you: the hope of glory!" (Colossians 1:27).

Christ himself is the power to live, love, and lead!

Christ's indwelling power provides tremendous promise and benefits. The Greek word *parakletos,* which Jesus uses in John 14:26 to describe the Holy Spirit, has various shades of meaning, yet all represent the same powerful reality of the role the Spirit plays in our lives: "advocate" (NIV), "helper" (ESV, NASB), "comforter" (KJV), "counselor" (HCSB). God's presence is always within us to compel, convict, comfort, and counsel. We are never alone, never without potential, never beyond grace, never not growing, and never needing to achieve anything that depends upon our own strength, intellect, or will.

It's no secret that despite this truth, many Christian leaders feel powerless. Our problem is not that the Spirit has left us, but that the hardships of life and leadership drain our awareness of the Holy Spirit's presence out of us. We forget he is within. When we do, we begin to operate in the flesh and to walk without dependence upon God. We start striving and mandating certain outcomes. Leadership becomes about us rather than about God and his people. In time we experience failure, frustration, or a kind of temporary, superficial success not born of God.

Consequently, the degree to which we are aware of and available to the Holy Spirit within is the degree to which he empowers us.

Awareness and Availability

Biblical leadership begins and ends in personal relationship to Christ. Every day, and in every step throughout the day, we are to "walk in the Spirit" (Romans 8:4; Galatians 5:16, 25), reminding ourselves that God's presence walks with us and resides in us. This dynamic, living reality allows a leader to gain peace, perspective, and strength throughout the course of leading others. It keeps him or her focused on what matters most, provides the ability for nonanxious response to obstacles, empowers an identity in Christ that transcends challenges to internal security, guides through times of hardship and difficult leadership decisions, and allows leaders to see with spiritual eyes the amazing possibilities that may come through faith and courage in Christ.

This constant consciousness of the Holy Spirit, however, does not come naturally. The sin nature seeks to make us live in our own power and walk independently from God. Therefore, in order to have an awareness of God, we must make ourselves available to God. *Awareness comes from availability.* This is true for any relationship. I can only become aware of the love and value of my marriage as I make myself available to my wife. The degree to which I walk in relationship with her is the degree to which I know her more and grow to love her more. In truth, the quality of any relationship is determined by our availability to it.

While this list is not exhaustive, there are a few specific channels through which we become available to God and aware of his work within us. Prayer, Sabbath-keeping, and the devotional study of God's Word are particularly important in the context of leadership.

When God gives his will, he also imparts the power to achieve it.
Biblical leadership begins and ends in
personal relationship to Christ.

Prayer

The true power of prayer begins with a disposition of the heart where we realize that we genuinely need God and believe that apart from him we can do nothing (John 15:5). This kind of desperation often results from the pain of trying to do things our own way. In time, and after some failure, we begin to truly desire God because we learn that we truly need him. This need creates a longing for heartfelt dialogue with the Father. Each day then begins with prayers of adoration, confession, thanksgiving, and requests made known to God (Philippians 4:6–7). It also leads to a lifestyle of constant prayer and dependence upon God, where throughout the day and in all situations we "pray without ceasing" (1 Thessalonians 5:17). The result is that we are always aware of God's presence because we are always turning to him and always speaking with him (John 15:4–5). As Brother Lawrence so beautifully states, "We need only to recognize God intimately present with us, to address ourselves to Him every moment, that we may beg His assistance for knowing His will in things doubtful, and for rightly performing those which we plainly see He requires of us, offering them to Him before we do them, and giving Him thanks when we have done."[59]

Prayer changes us in a way that goes beyond getting what we want from God. It allows us to stop in the midst of a driven, hurried existence and ponder the eternal. In prayer, we think about God's view of things and what he desires. With maturity we come to understand that prayer is not about getting God to see things our way or helping us do what we want, but instead it aligns our hearts with his wants and his will. Prayer allows us to transcend the temporal and fleshly and connect to a deeper power. When we pray for things and God grants the requests, we not only rejoice that in his sovereign will he has provided for what we've asked, but our hearts grow more confident in him and closer to him. God does not serve as a distant giver, i.e. a cosmic genie who grants our wishes. Instead, through prayer we grow in love and gratitude toward him through a submissive heart. When our requests are not granted as we hope, God has a way of changing our perspective about those requests, prompting us to change our prayers and giving us the strength to accept his will rather than demand ours. This is because we trust his heart and believe he knows best.

The power of prayer for leaders is that it joins our hearts to the Father's, allowing us to connect to the spiritual pulse of God and his activity in the world. It gives leaders a sense of God's work and how the leader could be used to influence God's people to join that work. In this way, a leader realizes calling and vision. Prayer secures the leader's thoughts, motives, actions, and decisions in the purposes of God. Prayer corrects the leader in thought and attitude, comforts the leader through trial and hardship, convicts the leader in what to do and how to do it, and compels the leader forward in faith and courage. Nothing is more important to the kind of spiritual leadership we are to give than personal, daily dialogue with God.

Sabbath-keeping

With the ongoing demands and pace of life, all of us must find rhythms by which to live. We must learn when to work, when to play, and when to rest and restore. This is particularly important for leaders because of the unique challenges associated with leadership, all of which can be draining spiritually and emotionally.

- *Leadership is a very public activity.* Leaders are out in front, pointing people to a future they might not fully understand or embrace. Leaders therefore must make decisions that impact others and at times are unpopular. Since this is true, leaders are a natural target for critique and questioning. They are often misunderstood. Their lives are lived before others, and much of all they do is on public display.
- *Leadership is people-intensive.* Let's face it—people can be the greatest reward of leadership and also the greatest frustration. People are sin-stained, messy and messed up, sometimes selfish and petty. Yet, they are the ones leaders are called to love and influence. This can be exhausting and emotionally draining.
- *Leadership means pressure.* Leaders are judged by outcomes. Their effectiveness is measured in terms of what is produced, not by what was intended or by how hard they work. While we must primarily see and measure ourselves as leaders by different standards (obedience to God, qualitative outcomes, etc.), those around us expect performance and results.
- *Leadership means always doing right.* Biblical leaders don't have the margin for mistakes that others enjoy. Others might get away with completely "losing it" emotionally, having fits of selfishness, or responding with anger when attacked. They might be able to make mistakes without consequence. Leaders can't. They cannot say what they want to say or do what they want to do. Christ compels us to act differently as leaders (1 Timothy 3:1–13). Too many are counting on us for something greater than what everyone else is doing. Additionally, when leaders do mess up, they must own their error and make it right in order to salvage trust. This is unlike others, who often don't have to admit wrong or face the results of their actions. An episode of anger, a major blunder, or

a self-serving decision, regardless of how justified, could ruin a leader and cause him or her to lose in one minute the credibility that took years to build. Leaders must always be "on their game," and there is little room for error.

- *Leadership often accompanies personal drive.* I know few in leadership who are lazy. Most instead are driven. They work hard and are willing to go above and beyond in order to be used by God to make a difference. However, this drivenness has a tendency to get out of control. Good, hard work turns into workaholism, and noble desires for godly outcomes develop into fleshly compulsions that must be followed at all costs. Leaders who are naturally driven are particularly susceptible to burnout and wipeout.

For all these reasons and more, leadership can be depleting physically, psychologically, emotionally, and spiritually, which then robs us of the power of Christ. That's why the principle of the Sabbath is so vitally important to anyone in a leadership role. Sabbath means not only a day of rest each week, but also the deeper notions of what God intended through that day of rest. The idea of the Sabbath includes finding *retreat*, engaging in *re-creation*, enjoying life-giving *relationships,* and experiencing activities that bring *restoration.* When put into practice, these dimensions of Sabbath help a leader last for the long term. Leadership is a marathon, not a sprint. Sabbath allows us strength to endure by helping us become aware and available to the living Christ within.

A Biblical Basis

Because the Sabbath is so important and yet so poorly practiced by many leaders, and because it has such potential benefits for leaders in particular, a biblical foundation and a thorough explanation of the practice is needed.

The word *Sabbath* is from the Hebrew word *Shabbat,* meaning "cessation" or "time of rest."[60] The text of the creation account provides the basis of all decrees for the practice of the Sabbath:

Thus the heavens and the earth were finished, and all the host of them. And on the seventh day God finished his work that he had done, and he rested on the seventh day from all his work that he had done. So God blessed the seventh day and made it holy, because on it God rested from all his work that he had done in creation. (Genesis 2:1–3)

No command for *us* to rest is given in this passage—only the fact that God rested. The word *Sabbath* is not even used. However, the seventh day is set apart and made holy because it is the day when God rested from his work. It is distinguished and sanctified by God himself.

The first occurrence of the term *Sabbath* and the first command for Israel to observe a Sabbath practice of any kind is found in Exodus 16:22–30. Here, Sabbath is mentioned in the context of manna provided by God in the wilderness wanderings. God provided twice as much on the sixth day and commanded his people to rest on the seventh day. Manna was not to be gathered on the seventh day because it was a "Sabbath to the Lord" (vv. 23, 26). Therefore, that which God did at creation is now transferred to his children. They are to rest on the seventh day.

Exodus 20 contains the Ten Commandments given to Moses for the people of Israel. The fourth command crystalizes the desire of God for his children to rest and restore on the seventh day. The command is clear and compelling:

Remember the Sabbath day, to keep it holy. Six days you shall labor, and do all your work, but the seventh day is a Sabbath to the Lord your God. On it you shall not do any work, you, or your son, or your daughter, your male servant, or your female servant, or your livestock, or the sojourner who is within your gates. For in six days the Lord made heaven and earth, the sea, and all that is in them, and rested on the seventh day. Therefore the Lord blessed the Sabbath day and made it holy. (Exodus 20:8–11)

It is interesting that the Israelites are not called upon to sanctify the Sabbath, but to protect it from becoming unsanctified. It was made holy by God at creation, but the way God's children conducted themselves by way of laboring on the seventh day could profane it before God.

The main idea for Sabbath is the cessation of work. The all-inclusive language ("you, or your son, or your daughter, your male servant, or your female servant, or your livestock, or the sojourner") signifies how important the termination of labor on this day was to God. The rest that was commanded here would eventually make way for worship to occur on the Sabbath (see the religious celebrations commanded in Leviticus and Numbers). In time, worship would become a part of this holy day, made possible because work was absent from it.

The Sabbath is distinguished and sanctified by God himself.

Why the correlation between the absence of work and holiness? Though by nature work is difficult in a sin-stained world (Genesis 2:17–19), it can be personally fulfilling as well as an extension of our worship to God. We may be called by God to certain professions and employ those callings through God-given gifts and abilities. These bring the possibility of nobility and godliness to labor. Some love work for these reasons. However, the very qualities that give work such potential for good may also bring harm. Work becomes harmful when love for it is taken to an extreme and when we lose the ability to step away from it. We then work too much, becoming preoccupied with work and what it produces. "There is happiness in the love of labor; there is misery in the love of gain."[61] Part of Satan's ploy is to take this good gift from God and pervert it. Work encroaches on every other dimension of life, not allowing us to separate from it. When this occurs, work even stands in the way of worship. Working on a day that is set apart for godly rest is the worship of work. In other words, we may worship work or worship God, but not both.

The principle of the Sabbath is God's ingenious command to help us draw boundaries around labor and live a healthy emotional and spiritual existence. The Sabbath means that once every week, for twenty-four hours we drop everything—every concern and every thought of every concern. When practiced properly, Sabbath allows the mind, body, and spirit to be restored and replenished.

True spiritual maturity requires the imitation of God. "God blessed the seventh day and made it holy, because on it God rested from all his work that he had done in creation" (Genesis 2:3). When we "sabbath," we do as God did. This is the essence of godliness.

Retreat

The dictionary provides several definitions of the word *retreat* that have particular application to Sabbath-keeping. Note especially number 4 below:

> Retreat [ree-treet]: (1) the forced or strategic withdrawal of an army or an armed force before an enemy; (2) the act of withdrawing, as into safety or privacy; retirement; seclusion; (3) a place of refuge, seclusion, or privacy; (4) an asylum, as for the insane.[62]

Retreat in this context means to escape normal, ongoing activity to engage in what is out of the ordinary and restorative. This is self-evidently a good thing. Yet, leaders often find it difficult to retreat for these reasons:

- *An addiction to achievement.* There are some who truly feel guilty when they relax. They see relaxation as selfish, irresponsible, and undisciplined. Thus, they have a preoccupying sense that there are always "better things" to do than unwind. When they sabbath, they believe they are not achieving. This, of course, is incorrect. They are achieving something of great value in regard to rest and connection to Christ—good for both the body and soul.

213

- *"There's still work to do."* Rarely do we finish in one week all the work we feel we need to finish. In fact, if you're a pastor, you know there is always something that can be done to make the church better. There are people to counsel and sick people to visit. There's always a need for more prayer, more strategic thinking, more relationship building, and more study for sermons—even on Sunday afternoons. After all, there are only a few days until the next sermon. Sunday comes with amazing regularity!
- *Demands of others.* Sometimes the demands of spouse, kids, family, and bosses preempt leaders of the choice to rest and restore. In this mind-set, we feel we have lost the ability to choose for ourselves what we do with our time. A sense of entrapment and loss of control sets in, which in turn leads to bitterness.
- *"Things will crash and burn if I step away."* We have a belief that if we are not engaged with work at all times, then the proverbial wheels will fall off. Things won't get done, people won't get taken care of, and life will be worse with the Sabbath than without it.

Yet the Bible is clear. God is not ambiguous in this command. We must sabbath in order to obey God, and in order to sabbath we must retreat from the life we live the other six days of the week.

Re-creation

Recreation means literally re-creating our selves. It means doing that which gives life in body, mind, and spirit, not that which drains it. Therefore, we must investigate and then affirm those activities that are not just different from the routine but also bring life back into us after six days of leadership depletes it.

Talk to anyone who regularly works out, whether by walking, running, bicycling, lifting weights, yoga, cross-training, or any other regular physical discipline, and they will tell you that the breakdown of muscle restores and rebuilds the body. A sense of physical re-creation is the result. The physical and mental benefits of such exercise are well established and need not be listed here. Spiritual benefit is also present, for as Paul would say, "Physical training is of some value" (1 Timothy 4:8) and "your bodies are temples of the Holy Spirit" (1 Corinthians 6:19). We do our souls well when we keep our bodies well. Some think Sabbath means lying on the couch watching TV all day on Sunday. Yet, as well as getting a good nap and plenty of rest, this day may legitimately include working the body differently than you do the rest of the week. Minor gardening, enjoyable handyman tasks, taking a hike or walk, going for a short run: such activities are not "work" provided they are different from your six-day-a-week routine and are not demanding or draining but are instead restorative. Physical activity on the Sabbath does not mean rigorously working out unless that is restorative to you. But lying dormant for hours upon hours rarely restores our bodies either. Sabbath is better experienced if we seek to recreate our bodies as well as rest them.

We recreate our minds by reading books, enjoying the arts, and engaging in thinking activities. Novels (books unrelated to work), movies, music, theater, art, museums: all create escapes that can renew the mind. Thinking activities such as chess, card games, puzzles, and board games can ignite parts of the mind that often lie dormant. Be careful, however—there are forms of mental activity that are not restorative at all. There is a difference between engaging the mind and merely entertaining it. While possibly harmless, some entertaining kinds of activities, including certain movies, video games, TV shows, music, and all the rest, don't lead to mental sharpening and restoration. How many times have you sat through five to six hours of mindless television and at the end of it said, "My, I feel alive and restored"? Not likely! Restoration comes by renewing our minds, not amusing them (Romans 12:2).

Recreating ourselves spiritually goes hand-in-hand with renewing ourselves in body and mind. We are, after all, whole selves and not merely parts. Therefore, beyond the disciplines of daily prayer and Bible study, on the Sabbath we should pursue that which helps us simply *enjoy* God. Worship and service should be spiritually restorative even for those in ministry. We all must discover some restorative dimension to worshiping on Sundays, even if we are the ones leading the time together. We should also, even in ministry, find joy in serving others and God on the Sabbath.

There are also outside-the-church pursuits that have great potential to restore spiritually. Art, poetry, and music can elicit spiritual emotions and comprehensions of God that are inspiring and healing. They allow us to ponder the amazing love of God, his character and might, and the multitude of spiritual blessings we possess. These are activities that move us to be joyous in God. Engaging nature by drinking in the sight of mountains or oceans, hiking a nature trail, or gazing at a flowery field or at the stars may cause us to consider the bigness of God and provide a deep, secure perspective for facing the challenges of life and leadership.

When I look at your heavens, the work of your fingers, the moon and the stars, which you have set in place, what is man that you are mindful of him, and the son of man that you care for him? Yet you have made him a little lower than the heavenly beings and crowned him with glory and honor. (Psalm 8:3–5)

Inspirational and restorative Sabbath-keeping, the kind that makes us aware of and more available to God, includes turning from the normal activity of working to the special activity of pondering God's work.

Transformation comes by renewing our minds, not amusing them.

Relationships

Certain people drain us. Other people restore life to us. This is a simple truth of life. On the Sabbath, leaders should surround themselves with people they actually enjoy. The recreating power of relationships is about leveraging time with those who help us live with peace and joy. On the Sabbath, spend time with family and friends, but do so differently than you do during the week. Time here should be purposed for life-giving conversations and family activities, not draining ones. Speak differently with your spouse and children on the Sabbath. Look at them with love on this day. Enjoy them and find joy in them. Rejoice in your heart for the gift of family that God has given you. If you spend time with friends, make sure they are restorative people, not difficult ones. The command "Remember the Sabbath day, to keep it holy" means taking steps to protect the day from ruin. This is your day and your time. Shelter it from anything or anyone that would make it unholy in the sense of violating its purpose of rest and renewal.

Restoration

Over time, leaders can develop a kind of weariness that cannot be cured with a good night's sleep. Spiritual fatigue is a weariness of the soul where the emotional and spiritual resources needed to sustain life and leadership are drained. Here, demand exceeds supply.

The Sabbath not only gives rest to our bodies, but when practiced properly, it brings restoration to our souls. On the Sabbath, labor ceases. But the Sabbath does not necessarily mean being finished with work. Rarely do we complete all our work in a given week. Instead, the Sabbath means being *free from the internal need to work*. The idea is to rest *as if* all your work is done.

The Sabbath separates us from the notion that the world can't survive without us. It serves as the antidote to the idea that I am indispensable to the world and that the things in the world, to which I give myself six days a week, are indispensable to me.

Partially quoting his father, Abraham Joshua Herschel aptly states,

We need the Sabbath in order to survive civilization: "Gallantly, ceaselessly, quietly man must fight for inner liberty" to remain independent from the enslavement of the material world. "Inner liberty depends upon being exempt from domination of things as well as from domination of people . . . This is our constant problem—how to live with people and remain free—how to live with things and remain independent.[63]

Time and money are two primary assets of our lives. Other than God and people, nothing is likely more important to us. There are amazing similarities in God's commands toward the management of our time and the management of our money. The Sabbath and the tithe stand as clear directives from a loving God in how to steward these precious resources:

- *Both imitate God.* In giving and in resting, I am doing what God himself did.
- *Both draw me close to God.* As I do what God did, I fellowship with him deeply, understanding his ways and identifying in relationship with him more.
- *Both are an antidote to the culture.* Tithing stands as an antidote to greed and materialism; Sabbath stands as an antidote to addictive work and indispensability.
- *Both bless me in return.* The irony is that though I give away my money in tithing and give away my time in Sabbath, I have enough money and enough time for living. God provides in return so that by giving I receive and my needs are adequately supplied. It is amazing to see how efficient and effective my time becomes on the other six days of the week when I sabbath on the seventh. The same is true for my money when I tithe.
- *Both set my priorities in the proper place.* By tithing and keeping the Sabbath, I do not allow my money and time to manage me. I instead manage them. This keeps them in proper perspective for healthy living. The disciplines stop the encroaching power of time and money and the obsession associated with each. Tithing and the Sabbath keep time and money from becoming idols of worship.

- *Both are proportional.* Sabbath is one-seventh of my week; tithing is one-tenth of my money. While all my time and all my money are his, I practically give to God for a specific purpose in proportion to all he has given me.
- *Both are systematic.* I give from the first of my income and from the last of my week.
- *Both are sacrificial.* Time and money are precious, limited resources and therefore are not easily given to God, which is exactly why God requires them.
- *Both reveal my level of trust in God.* Tithing and Sabbath-keeping are a constant, concrete reminder that God is the owner of all and that I can trust him with the most important portions of my life. They remind me that he is the provider and will make up anything I might lack through giving and keeping the Sabbath. To reject the Sabbath or refuse to tithe means not trusting or believing God in the most practical sense. Not giving and not keeping Sabbath are practical atheism. When I give and when I rest as God prescribed, I show my trust in him, my belief that he knows best, and my dependence upon him for all of life.

The Sabbath, therefore, is an act of faith. It means trusting God with the leadership of our organization in our absence; trusting him with our need for rest (whether we think we need it or not); and trusting him with the need for consistent, weekly worship. The Sabbath is not a suggestion. It is not a nice recommendation from God. It is a clear command. But it is a command from a loving Father who seeks the best for his children and who desires for leaders to experience authentic power from within.

Stay in the secret place till the surrounding noises begin to fade out of your heart and a sense of God's presence envelops you. Listen for the inward Voice till you learn to recognize it. Give yourself to God and then be what and who you are without regard to what others think.[64]

The Devotional Study of God's Word

My wife and I routinely have a date night. But that routine is not for the purpose of saying that we've had a date night as good couples are supposed to do. Instead, its purpose and practice is to allow us to grow more in love with each other. If we have a date night and do not achieve that end, we have practiced the law of dating without fulfilling its spirit. The date night provides a structure and discipline in which we may achieve a purpose. It is a channel through which love is expressed and grown in our marriage.

The discipline of reading God's Word is similar. All of us have been told that we need to have a daily quiet time that includes reading the Bible. That's what "good Christians" do. However, the discipline of reading God's Word should grow a spirit of love for God in our hearts, not fulfill a legalistic requirement. We do not practice it so we can simply check it off the list. Nor do we practice it simply to gain information about God, just as I do not take my wife out merely to gain more data about her. Any knowledge we acquire from the Bible should transfer into a deeper appreciation and awareness of God. As Paul said, "The goal of our instruction is love from a pure heart and a good conscience and a sincere faith" (1 Timothy 1:5).

Reading God's word devotionally instead of legalistically, clinically, or only for knowledge's sake means keeping our hearts focused on the intended outcome. This is not to say that all reading and study of the Bible should be devotional in nature. Formal, theological study of God's Word for knowledge and insight is greatly beneficial to spiritual development and sermon preparation. But this should not take place at the expense of loving relationship to God through his Word. As Michelle DeRusha writes, "It's tempting to get lost in the study, to turn to books and study groups and classes, to know all about God but not know God himself, to read about the Bible rather than read the Bible itself."[65]

If we read the Bible without growing in love for God,
we have practiced the law of devotion without fulfilling its spirit.

The ways to read the Bible that place us in a context for loving God include:

- *Reading it personally.* This means allowing God to speak to me *personally* through the words. Understanding the meaning of God's Word means first understanding its meaning in its original context and to its original hearers— but that's not end of the study of God's Word. The Bible is not only about the people, time, and situations in the day it was written. Those meanings also apply to us. Personally applying God's Word to the deepest and most practical dimensions of our lives allows us to grow more in love with God.

- *Reading it prayerfully.* This means allowing God to speak to you in the prompting of your heart and then speaking back to God as you read. This also includes praying and asking the Holy Spirit for guidance, understanding, and illumination about the Scripture; praying the actual words of the biblical text when possible; and praying for others as you think of them while reading.

- *Reading it authentically.* Being authentic in the reading of God's Word means being willing to put it into practice. As we read the Bible, we pause now and again, asking ourselves whether we really live by these words and whether in our hearts we actually believe the words just read. To read the Word of God without a deep, authentic desire to put it into practice is self-deceit. As James said, "Do not merely listen to the word, and so deceive yourselves. Do what it says" (James 1:22).

Reading God's Word devotionally allows it to seep into our hearts and thereby protects us from a merely clinical, superficial approach to it. This makes God's Word alive to us and moves us to see God through it. When this occurs, we become more aware of the Father and more available to him, and we possess a greater sense of his power and presence within. As the prophet Jeremiah describes it, when God's Word is placed deeply within us, it has tremendous potential to change us, arrest us with joy, and help us recognize God's power and our place in relationship to him:

Your words were found and I ate them,
And Your words became for me a joy and the delight of my heart;
For I have been called by Your name,
O Lord God of hosts.
(Jeremiah 15:16)

God Develops Power to Lead

Experiencing God's power involves many dynamics. At a base level, it requires that the leader engage in a process of growth and development. The experience of Christ's power in leadership is not bequeathed but developed.

We may read about leaders in the Scripture and tend to think they were born with or simply endowed with traits of faith, courage, and other qualities for effectiveness. They seem to be heroic naturally. This is an inaccurate understanding.

Abraham was called to leave his homeland and be used by God to create a nation. He is known as the "father of our faith" and is hailed as a faith hero and a man used by God for a great purpose. But Abraham's faith came in seed form and developed over time through failure as well as success. Though told to leave his family behind, he initially compromised God's call by bringing along his nephew, Lot (Genesis 12:4). When God's promise of a son was delayed, Abraham and Sarah took matters into their own hands and devised a scheme outside of God's provision by which a son could be born (Genesis 16). When put in a pressured situation, Abraham lied about the nature of his relationship with Sarah (Genesis 20:1–2). All are examples of a lack of belief. Yet ultimately, after years of wavering in matters of faith, Abraham learned that he could indeed trust God with his all. He was finally convinced. His faith that God could be trusted was epitomized by his willingness to sacrifice his son Isaac on the altar at Mount Moriah (Genesis 22).

Power in leadership is not bequeathed but developed.

Moses was a fugitive and recluse when God came calling. He was raised in wealth and royalty but escaped Egypt after committing a murder. By the time the burning bush appeared, he had spent forty years in retreat, tending sheep with his father-in-law. Yet God called him to go back to Egypt and be used to free people who had been in slavery for four hundred years. Moses was reluctant, to say the least, and he offered many excuses not to go (Exodus 3–4). After some convincing, this man of self-doubt, armed only with God's presence, confronted the most powerful person on the planet. Great miracles occurred, and God's people were finally out of Egypt. Yet, through a long experience of wilderness wanderings due to the people's lack of faith, Moses's own anger and impatience often got the best of him (Exodus 32, Numbers 16). Moses's fury even disqualified him from leading the people into the Promised Land (Numbers 20:1–13). In the end, however, this man troubled with doubt and anger was more greatly characterized by courage and faith (Hebrews 11:24–27). He was used by God to achieve an amazing purpose and to influence others for God's glory.

This picture of flawed but growing leaders holds throughout the Bible. The apostle Peter was known for speaking words of great faith and loyalty, yet when the time of testing came, he was unable to follow through (Matthew 16:16, 26:33, 26:69–75). Peter's problem was not one of sincerity. His was a problem of integrity—he lacked the strength of character to practice in his life what he proclaimed with his lips. Jesus tried to warn him of this lack of character when he predicted Peter's denials (Matthew 26:30–34). Yet, as with us, Peter had to learn through experience what he was unwilling and unable to learn through instruction. At the moment of his third denial of Jesus, he was awakened to the stark truth that he was not the person he had claimed to be. At that point he had to own his lack of courage and admit what was painfully true about him. But failure is never final in Christ! Jesus was about changing Peter from within.

In John 21:15–19, after his resurrection, Jesus gave Peter an opportunity to once again recklessly boast about his devotion: "Simon, son of John, do you love me more than these?" (v. 15). This is an obvious reference back to Peter's claim to remain devoted to Jesus when others would not (Mark 14:29). Peter does not respond in kind. Rather than say, "Yes. I love you more than these," he replies humbly, accurately, and honestly— "Yes, Lord; you know that I love you." Three times this exchange occurs, symbolizing the forgiveness and restoration of Peter upon his three denials of Jesus. The Lord uses this exchange as a way of confirming the shameful reality to Peter while at the same time restoring him to usefulness in ministry and purpose for the future. "Feed my sheep" he told him in v. 17, and "after saying this he said to him, 'Follow me'" (v 19).

Peter's future effectiveness as a leader in ministry was dependent upon his walking through this experience, owning his lack of integrity, and learning from it. Afterward, he spoke boldly and courageously for the name of Christ and suffered because of it (Acts 2:14–41, 3:12–26, 5:29–32, 4:1–3, 5:17–42, 12:1–5).

Failure is never final in Christ!

The Bible likewise provides many insights into the internal struggles as well as the external successes of the apostle Paul. Known as Saul before his conversion, he was obsessed with achievement in the Jewish religious power structure (Acts 7:59–8:3, Galatians 1:13–14, Philippians 3:4–11). As a powerful Pharisee, he gained notoriety, privilege, praise, and wealth. Through a process that began with a blinding light from heaven (Acts 9:3), Paul's identity and destiny were changed through Christ. Once basing his life upon external achievements, he had now been made righteous through faith and secure solely in Christ.

Yet when we look closely at the Christian experience of the apostle Paul, we see intense struggles with the power of sin (Romans 7), a misplaced and severe dispute with the encourager Barnabas (Acts 15:36–41), constant conflict with opponents of the gospel (Galatians 1:6–9, Philippians 3:2, 1 Timothy 1:18–20, 2 Timothy 4:14), tremendous sufferings (2 Corinthians 12:23–33), and a troubling "thorn in the flesh" that recurrently tormented him (2 Corinthians 12:7). Life and leadership were difficult for Paul. But these sufferings and struggles did not stand in opposition to his ability to influence others. Rather, they were inextricably tied to Paul's growth as a believer first and then as a leader. Through these experiences, and only through them, God was able to grow Paul and employ him as the greatest missionary in the history of the Christian faith.

In every instance, leaders in the Bible were far from perfect, and their power to lead grew over a period of time through pain, challenge, and even failure. What made these leaders heroic was their engagement with God in a lifelong process. This process was filled with failure and success alike, including times when they questioned and even disobeyed God. Their journey to ultimately fulfill God's will was characterized by multiple years of growth. This growth was not immediate, and it did not take place in a linear fashion. At times they advanced through courage and submission; at other times they retreated in reluctance, fear, and rebellion. In the end, however, two things made them successful: their overriding willingness to grow and learn and the fact that they didn't give up.

Those who want to be used by God as leaders must commit themselves to a lifelong pilgrimage of development characterized by humility and teachability. They must also determine that they will never quit in following God in this journey.

Sanctification and Leadership

The primary calling of the biblical leader is to know and love Christ. It is our foremost passion (Philippians 3:10). In a biblical context, to be a leader is to be an authentic disciple of Jesus. Biblical leadership means for leaders to first encounter the power of Christ and then express the power of Christ. The apostle Paul summarized this thought when he said,

"Follow my example, as I follow the example of Christ" (Philippians 4:9). Paul implies that effective, Christ-honoring leadership is not first about leading, but about following. If biblical leaders are called to give Christ to others (as they certainly are), then they as leaders must follow him, love him, and serve him first. You cannot give to others what you do not possess. Indeed, we are called to behold for ourselves the glory of God and then to reflect it to others. This is to lead!

Our primary calling is to know and love Christ.
To be a biblical leader is first to be an authentic disciple of Jesus.

Because this is true, as one grows as a believer, one has the potential to grow as a leader. In truth, we do not grow as biblical leaders unless we grow spiritually. This means the process of sanctification and the process of leader development go hand in hand. They are concurrent, inextricably tied, and they affect each other significantly. For example, as we grow into Christlikeness, the traits associated with such development—humility, submission, confession, followership, trust in God, and the rest—all create a capacity within us to be used by the Father as leaders. God is able to empower and employ someone fully submitted to him! Likewise, the desire for holiness creates a humble, teachable, and willing person— characteristics necessary for potential leaders to learn leadership competencies that do not come naturally, or to continue to learn and grow through trial and conflict. Personal holiness defies prideful leadership.

At the same time, God uses leadership, with its associated callings and challenges, as tools to make us more Christlike. In fact, the things that are a part of the function of leadership—perhaps most especially the difficult things—become the very instruments used by God to grow us in faith and holiness. In this sense, leadership accomplishes a godly purpose *within* the leader, not simply one *through* him or her. The challenges of leadership get us out of our comfort zone, create disequilibrium, and cause us to question the adequacy of our own skills. These circumstances lead to faith in Christ rather than in self. Indeed, *the God who seeks to do a work through us is he who seeks to do a work in us.* This we find true for every leader mentioned in the Bible.

As J. Oswald Sanders stated,

> It has been said that in achieving His world-purpose, God's method has always been a man. Not necessarily a noble man, or a brilliant man, but always a man with capacity for a growing faith. Granted this, there appears to be no limit to the pains God is willing to take in his training. He is limited by neither heredity nor environment.[66]

Consequently, biblical leadership—being able to be powerfully used by God to influence others for his glory—is not primarily about a leader's *ability*. Rather, it is first about his or her *availability* to God—the willingness to grow in faith and follow Christ fully. The disciples may have not been the sharpest of people. They certainly were not the most educated nor the most externally qualified. They did one thing, however, that many in their day didn't. They said yes to Jesus. They followed Christ when he called. Leaders today similarly say to God, "I'm willing. The answer is yes. Now God, what is the question?"

In Conclusion

Worldly leaders operate in their own strength and in their own wisdom, and they may be able to accomplish good and even noble things. Even Christian leaders set out to do great things *for* God. Yet in truth God doesn't want us nor need us to act on his behalf. He seeks to do something great *through* us by means of a living faith in him.

Biblical leadership produces eternal results because it comes from a different source. It is not based upon the world's wisdom or the meager human resources of the leader. These sources can only accomplish what can be explained in natural and human ways and through the limited skills of the leader. By contrast, the inner fuel, guide, and force at work for the biblical leader is the very power of Christ.

A real, living faith in God is his highest desire for us as his creation. "And without faith it is impossible to please him, for whoever would draw near to God must believe that he exists and that he rewards those who seek him" (Hebrews 11:6). Leadership and its effects, as God intended, are only byproducts of a life yielded to him. We don't love God in order to lead better. We love God because we love him. Healthy and effective leadership is just one of the possible manifestations of a sincere love and faith.

While loving the Father and living in responsive faith to him is not pursued for the purpose of being an effective biblical leader, this relationship *is* a prerequisite to it. The more we love Jesus, the more capacity we have to be used by him. Therefore, the quality of our leadership is contingent upon the quality of our relationship with Christ. Nothing is more important.

When Christ is first, he accomplishes through the humble, willing leader that which can only be ascribed to God's ability. In the end, the leader sees limitless possibilities for what can be achieved. When the task is complete, it is God, not the leader, who receives the credit. We continue to give God the glory; he will continue to give us his power.

"For this reason I kneel before the Father, from whom his whole family in heaven and on earth derives its name. I pray that out of his glorious riches he may strengthen you with power through his Spirit in your inner being, so that Christ may dwell in your hearts through faith. And I pray that you, being rooted and established in love, may have power, together with all the saints, to grasp how wide and long and high and deep is the love of Christ, and to know this love that surpasses knowledge—that you may be filled to the measure of all the fullness of God. Now to him who is able to do immeasurably more than all we ask or imagine, according to his power that is at work within us, to him be glory in the church and in Christ Jesus throughout all generations, for ever and ever! Amen." (Ephesians 3:14–21, NIV 1984)

Chapter Review Questions

1. What is the significance of the resurrection to empowered leadership today?
2. This chapter claims that God gives the power to accomplish his will. How does this set Christianity apart from world religions or secular success structures?
3. List several translations of the Greek *parakletos* that illuminate the role of the Spirit in our lives.
4. Do you agree that our awareness and availability will determine the degree to which the Spirit empowers us? Why or why not?
5. List at least five ways in which a regular prayer life effects inner transformation.
6. List the four key activities of Sabbath and describe their combined result.
7. Describe the inherent goodness of work and the dangers that also attend it. How does Sabbath allow us to experience the goodness of work without succumbing to its dangers? Explain.
8. Does addiction to achievement prevent you from practicing and enjoying Sabbath? What change of perspective or priority is needed to see value in this practice?
9. List the similarities between Sabbath-keeping and tithing. How do these disciplines make us more aware and available to God?
10. What are three ways to read the Bible that place us in a context for loving God?
11. In what sense can sufferings and struggles be said to increase our ability to influence others?
12. What is the primary calling of the biblical leader?
13. Describe the confluence of growth as a believer and growth as a leader.

Notes

1. Pew Research Center. "Nones on the Rise." Accessed 9/11/14 from http://www.pewforum.org/2012/10/09/nones-on-the-rise/. October 9, 2012

2. George Barna and David Kinneman, eds. *Churchless: Understanding Today's Unchurched and How to Connect with Them.* Carol Stream, IL: Tyndale, 2014.

3. George Barna. *The Power of Vision: Discover and Apply God's Vision for Your Life & Ministry.* Venture, CA: Regal Publishing, 2009.

4. R.H. Welch. *Church Administration: Creating Efficiency for Effective Ministry.* Nashville, TN: Broadman & Holman Publishers, 2005. p. vii.

5. C.A. Schwartz. *Natural Church Development.* St. Charles, IL: ChurchSmart Resources, 1996.

6. The Association of Theological Schools. *Annual Data Tables* (2010–2011). http://www.ats.edu/. Includes Fuller Theological Seminary, Southwestern Baptist Theological Seminary, Southeastern Baptist Theological Seminary, Southern Seminary, Dallas Theological Seminary, Gordon-Conwell Seminary, Trinity Seminary, Asbury Seminary, Golden Gate Theological Seminary, New Orleans Baptist Theological Seminary, and Bethel Seminary.

7. Denham Grierson, *Transforming a People of God,* Melbourne: Joint Board of Christian Education, 1984. p. 18.

8. Charles C. Ryrie. *Basic Theology: A Popular Systematic Guide to Understanding Biblical Truth.* Chicago, IL.: Moody Publishers, 1999. p. 13.

9. Thomas E. Cronin, as cited in Lovett H. Weems, *Church Leadership: Vision, Team, Culture, Integrity.* Nashville, TN: Abingdon Press, 1993. p. 16.

10. Peter G. Northouse. *Leadership: Theory and Practice.* Thousand Oaks, CA: Sage, 2006. p. 170.

11. Gary Yukl. *Leadership in organizations.* 5th ed. Upper Saddle River, NJ: Prentice Hall, 2002. p. 253.

12. James MacGregor Burns. *Leadership.* New York: Harper & Row, 1978. p. 2.

13. Warren Bennis and Burt Nanus. *Leaders: The Strategies for Taking Charge.* New York: Harper Collins, 1997. p. 4.

14. Peter Drucker, as quoted in John Pearson, *Mastering the Management Buckets: 20 Critical Competencies for Leading Your Business or Nonprofit,* 2008. pp. 67-75.

15. John C. Maxwell. *The 21 Irrefutable Laws of Leadership.* Nashville, TN: Thomas Nelson, 2007. p. 11.

16. Gary Yukl. *Leadership in organizations.* 5th ed. Upper Saddle River, NJ: Prentice Hall, 2002. p. 8

17. Peter G. Northouse. *Leadership: Theory and Practice.* Thousand Oaks, CA: Sage, 2006. p. 3.

18. Ken Blanchard. *Leading at a Higher Level.* Upper Saddle River, NJ: Prentice Hall, 2007, p. xvi.

19. James M. Kouzes and Barry Z. Posner. *The Leadership Challenge*. San Francisco, CA: Jossey-Bass, 2007. p. 14.

20. Stephen Covey. "The Leader Formula: 4 Things That Make a Great Leader." *www.StephenCovey.com*. Accessed 18 May 2012. http://www.stephencovey.com/blog/?p=6

21. A.W. Tozer. "The Menace of the Religious Movie", Accessed May 21, 2015. http://www.biblebb.com/files/tozermovie.htm

22. Warren Bennis. *On Becoming a Leader*. Reading, MA: Addison-Wesley Publishing Co. Inc., 1989. p. 5.

23. Shakespeare, William. *History of Henry IV, Part II*. Accessed July 10, 2014. http://www.opensourceshakespeare.org/

24. Schein, E. H. *Organizational Culture and Leadership*. San Francisco, CA: Jossey-Bass Publishers, 1987. p. 319.

25. Strong, J. (2001). *Enhanced Strong's Lexicon*. Bellingham, WA: Logos Bible Software.

26. Zodhiates, S. (2000). *The complete word study dictionary: New Testament* (electronic ed.). Chattanooga, TN: AMG Publishers.

27. Strong, J. (2001). *Enhanced Strong's Lexicon*. Bellingham, WA: Logos Bible Software.

28. Swanson, J. (1997). *Dictionary of Biblical Languages with Semantic Domains: Greek (New Testament)* (electronic ed.). Oak Harbor: Logos Research Systems, Inc.

29. Henri Nouwen, *In the Name of Jesus; Reflections on Christian Leadership* (New York: Crossroad, 1989. pp. 81-82.

30. Abraham Joshua Heschel. *The Sabbath.* Farrar, Strous and Giroux, New York. 1951. p. 3.

31. Jimmy Draper. "The Essential Element of Christian Leadership". Accessed May 13, 2015. http://ftc.co/resource-library/blog-entries/the-essential-element-of-christian-leadership.

32. Lovett H. Weems. *Church Leadership: Vision, Team, Culture, Integrity.* Nashville, TN: Abingdon Press, 1993, 65.

33. Peter Drucker. "Managing for Business Effectiveness." *Harvard Business Review,* May 1963. pp. 53–60.

34. Antoine De Saint-Exupery, as cited in D. Bray, *A Willful Volunteer: Examining Conscience in an Unconscious World.* Lincoln, NE. iUniverse, 2001. p. 71.

35. Edgar Schein, *Organizational Culture and Leadership* (San Francisco: Jossey-Bass, 2010), 9.

36. John F. Kennedy. Address in the Assembly Hall at Paulskirche. Frankfurt, Germany. June 25, 1963. (Accessed 12.13.14 at http://www.presidency.ucsb.edu/ws/?pid=9303)

37. Max Dupree, *Leadership is an Art* (New York: Dell Publishing, 1989), 11.

38. Charles F. Kettering as cited in Richard C. Dorf and Thomas H. Byers, *Technology Ventures: From Idea to Enterprise* (New York: McGraw Hill, 2005), 27.

39. Andy Stanley, *Visioneering* (Colorado Springs: Multnomah Books, 1999), 16.

40. Revised from Maxwell's quote in John Maxwell, *Thinking for a Change: 11 Ways Highly Successful People Approach Life and Work* (New York: Warner Books, 2003), 47.

41. Walt Kelly, *Pogo: We Have Met The Enemy And He Is Us.* 2nd edition. (New York: Simon & Schuster, 1972)

42. J. Swanson, *Dictionary of Biblical Languages with Semantic Domains: Greek (New Testament).* Electronic ed. (Oak Harbor, WA: Logos Research Systems, 1997)

43. See the following: Irwin G. Sarason, Barbara R. Sarason, and Edward N. Shearin, "Social support as an individual difference variable: Its stability, origins, and relational aspects." *Journal of Personality and Social Psychology,* Vol 50(4), Apr 1986, 845–855. Wm. Matthew Bowler and Daniel J. Brass, "Relational correlates of interpersonal citizenship behavior: A social network perspective," *Journal of Applied Psychology,* Vol 91(1), Jan 2006, 70–82. Susan R. Madsen, Duane Miller, and Cameron R. John, "Readiness for organizational change: Do organizational commitment and social relationships in the workplace make a difference?" *Human Resource Development Quarterly,* Vol 16 (2), Summer 2005, 213–234.

44. As cited in Stephen R. Covey, *The 7 Habits of Highly Effective People: Powerful Lessons in Personal Change.* Deluxe Edition. New York: Simon & Schuster, 2013. 108.

45. K.S. Wuest, *Wuest's Word Studies from the Greek New Testament: For the English Reader.* Grand Rapids: Eerdmans, 1997, c 1984. 110.

46. C. Gore, H.L. Goudge, and A. Guillame, eds. *A New Commentary on Holy Scripture including the Apocrypha.* New York: Abington Press, 1955. 52.

47. Wuest, 113.

48. Ibid., 112.

49. Ibid.

50. Scott Peck, *The Road Less Traveled: A New Psychology of Love, Traditional Values and Spiritual Growth.* New York: Touchstone, 1978. 82.

51. Ian I. Mitroff and Elizabeth A. Denton, *A Spiritual Audit of Corporate America: A Hard Look at Spirituality, Religion, and Values in the Workplace.* San Francisco, CA: Jossey-Bass, 1999. 155.

52. Denis Waitley, *Empires of the Mind: Lessons to Lead and Succeed in a Knowledge-Based World.* New York: Morrow, 1994. 161.

53. James M. Kouzes and Barry Z. Posner, *The Leadership Challenge,* 3rd edition. San Francisco, CA: Jossey-Bass, 2002. 375–376.

54. Max DePree, *Attributes of Leaders.* Executive Excellence, 1997. 14(4), 8.

55. Stephen R. Covey, *The Seven Habits of Highly Effective People.* New York: Simon and Schuster, 1990. 199.

56. James A. Autrey, *Love and Profit: The Art of Caring Leadership.* New York: Avon Books, 1992. 30–32.

57. G. Graen and J.F. Cashman, "A Role Making Model of Leadership in Formal Organizations: A Developmental Approach," in J.G. Hunt and L.L. Larson (eds), *Leadership Frontiers* (Kent, OH: Kent State University Press, 1975). F. Dansereau, Jr, G. Graen, and W.J. Haga, "A vertical dyad linkage approach to leadership within formal organizations: A longitudinal investigation of the role making process," *Organizational Behavior and Human Performance, 13,* 1975 (pp 46–78). H. Risan, "Dyadic Relationships for Leaders in Facility Management," *International Journal of Facility Management,* Vol.4 (1), 2013 (pps 1–10).

58. S. Zodhiates, *The Complete Word Study Dictionary: New Testament,* electronic ed. Chattanooga, TN: AMG Publishers, 2000.

59. Brother Lawrence, *Practicing the Presence of God.* Holicong, PA: Wildside Press, 2010. 10.

60. E.J. Young and F.F. Bruce, "Sabbath," in D.R.W. Wood, I.H. Marshall, A.R. Millard, J.I. Packer, and D.J. Wiseman (Eds.), *New Bible Dictionary,* 3rd ed. Leicester, England; Downers Grove, IL: InterVarsity Press, 1996. 1032.

61. Abraham Joshua Herschel, *The Sabbath.* New York: Farrar, Strauss, and Giroux Publishers, 2005. 3.

62. http://dictionary.reference.com/browse/retreat. Accessed April 17, 2015

63. Herschel, 77.

64. A.W. Tozer, *Tozer on Christian Leadership: A 366-day devotional.* Camp Hill, PA: WingSpread, 2001. 128–129.

65. Michelle DeRusha, *Spiritual Misfit: A Memoir of Uneasy Faith*. New York: Convergent Books, 2014. 207.

66. J. Oswald Sanders, *Robust in Faith*. Chicago, IL: Moody Press, 1965. 9.